SHORT BIKE RIDES®
IN NORTH CAROLINA

D0873013

Help Us Keep This Guide Up to Date

Every effort has been made by the author and editors to make this guide as accurate and useful as possible. However, many things can change after a guide is published—establishments close, phone numbers change, hiking trails are rerouted, facilities come under new management, etc.

We would love to hear from you concerning your experiences with this guide and how you feel it could be made better and be kept up to date. While we may not be able to respond to all comments and suggestions, we'll take them to heart, and we'll also make certain to share them with the author. Please send your comments and suggestions to the following address:

The Globe Pequot Press
Reader Response/Editorial Department
P.O. Box 480
Guilford, CT 06437

Or you may e-mail us at:

editorial@globe-pequot.com

Thanks for your input, and happy travels!

Short Bike Rides® Series

Short Bike Rides® in North Carolina

By

Judi Lawson Wallace

Guilford, Connecticut

Copyright © 1997 by Judi Lawson Wallace

All rights reserved. No part of this book may be reproduced or transmitted in any form by any means, electronic or mechanical, including photocopying and recording, or by any information storage and retrieval system, except as may be expressly permitted by the 1976 Copyright Act or by the publisher. Requests for permission should be made in writing to The Globe Pequot Press, P.O. Box 480, Guilford, Connecticut 06437.

Short Bike Rides is a registered trademark of The Globe Pequot Press
Photo of Blue Ridge Parkway by David Pounds; all other photos by Judi Lawson Wallace

Library of Congress Cataloging-in-Publication Data
Wallace, Judi Lawson.
  Short bike rides in North Carolina / by Judi Lawson Wallace.—1st ed.
      p.   cm. — (Short bike rides series)
  ISBN 0-7627-0212-5
  1. Bicycle touring—North Carolina—Guidebooks. 2. North Carolina—Guidebooks. I. Title. II. Series
  GV1045.5.N75W35   1998
  917.5604'43—dc21   97-48474
                                                                CIP

Manufactured in the United States of America
First Edition/Second Printing

For Bruce—the world's best "sagwaggie" and my favorite traveling companion

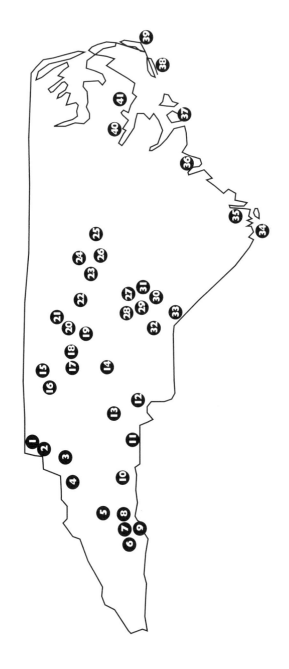

Contents

Coast

Introduction

North Carolina is the perfect place for bicycling: lots of sunshine, moderate temperatures even in winter, four gorgeous seasons, beautiful scenery, and varied terrain. Historic and cultural attractions complement its natural beauty and offer something for everyone. From stock car racing to opera, Carowinds to Old Salem, lounging on the beach or hiking in the mountains, you'll find lots to enjoy in the Old North State.

Frequently called the Variety Vacationland, the Tar Heel State stretches several hundred miles from the Blue Ridge Mountains and the Great Smoky Mountains of the Appalachian chain through the Piedmont and the Sandhills to the Coastal Plain. Its highest point, Mt. Mitchell (north of Asheville) rises to 6,684 feet and is also the tallest peak in the eastern United States. Sea level at the coast is the state's lowest point. With 52,586 square miles, North Carolina ranks twenty-eighth in size among all the states. In population, which is more than 7 million, the state ranks tenth.

Since the establishment of the North Carolina Bicycle Program in 1974, the state has developed many wonderful routes and programs to attract cyclists to its well-maintained highway system. The first of these was the Murphy-to-Manteo route for the Mountains to Sea System. With the assistance and oversight of the state office, many local areas have also produced maps and guides for bicycle tourists, some of which served as the basis for tours in this book.

North Carolina's climate is almost ideal for cycling year-round. Humid, hot summer days make it prudent to start very early to avoid the hottest times of the day. But spring and fall are spectacular anywhere in the state. Except for the mountains, the winters are generally mild enough for cyclists to get in some miles. And, as though the natural wonders weren't enough, the North Carolina Department of Transportation (DOT) was a leader in planting expanses of wildflowers along certain roadways.

In North Carolina you can find just about anything you'd like to see: sand dunes, rugged mountain peaks, lush valleys, historic towns, quiet forests, islands, lakes, and red clay. You can start in the east where the flat terrain makes pedaling easy—although the winds are sometimes very strong—move inland to the Sandhills and Piedmont for more rolling terrain, and then head to the mountains for some real challenges. But believe it or not, even the mountains have their share of lovely, flat rides beside rivers.

For more information on North Carolina, contact the Division of Travel and Tourism, 430 North Salisbury Street, Raleigh, NC 27611. The phone number is (919) 733–4171 in Raleigh or (800) 847–4862 outside Raleigh.

About the Rides

What a difficult task—selecting only forty-one rides for this book! There could easily have been twice that many. So I've done my best—fallible as that may be—to choose a wide variety of rides, both in length and in terrain. I surveyed all the bike clubs in the state, asking for their recommendations, but mainly I relied on my own cycling experience and knowledge of the state. Some of the state's more scenic areas have several routes because they have made special efforts to welcome cyclists and encourage their motorists to share the road.

These tours include a mix of urban and rural, some of which followed—either partially or completely—signed bike routes. Where that happens, the signed bike route numbers are included along with the road name and state road numbers. Although most of the rides are loops, some are out and back to minimize the distance where there are limited alternative routes.

The rides range in length from slightly more than 5 miles to slightly more than 40 miles and offer something for every ability level, from beginners to advanced veteran cyclists. Some of the rides are ideal for families, but children riding on their own should probably be at least ten years old to handle the intersections safely. All the rides are on paved roads and were selected with touring bikes in mind. For some, there are optional side trips or alternative routes you can select, depending on your level of energy and experience.

Each ride includes a map; information on length, pedaling time, traffic, terrain, things to see, where to find food, and a general description of the ride; detailed mile-by-mile directions; and directions to the starting point. The pedaling times are based on a leisurely pace; yours will likely vary according to your pedaling speed and the number of stops you make.

The rides are numbered, beginning with those in the mountains and moving across the state to the coast, which was pretty much the order in which I researched the rides. Most of the rides start from public attractions, state parks, or college campuses. The directions for each ride also give suggestions about where to park, if it isn't obvious.

Enjoying the Rides
Using the Maps

Please note that the maps are not drawn to scale and, by necessity, don't include every street or road in an area. Interstate highways are indicated with the letter I hyphenated with the number—for example, I–26. U.S. highways are denoted with the initials U.S. and the highway number—for example, U.S. 421. State highways carry the initials *NC,* hyphenated with the highway number—for example, NC–194. In North Carolina, all the rural roads have been given names to help emergency services more quickly find those who need help. In addition, the state's secondary roads continue to use the designation SR and a four-digit number. In some locations, these state road numbers may be difficult to find. On the green-and-white road signs, they are frequently—but not always—placed on the sign along with the road's name. In some highway divisions and counties, however, you may have to look for black and white numbers shown vertically on the posts for stop signs or other directional signs at intersections.

The maps give both the name and the secondary road number where both were available. The directions indicate if a sign was missing at the time of research, although there's no guarantee that all other signs are in place. Where optional rides are available, the directions are given with the overall ride directions. Because the maps give only the basic streets and highways, it's important to follow carefully the "Directions at a glance," which will point out difficulties that might not be apparent on the map.

The Right Equipment

One of the best things about cycling is that you don't need a lot of fancy gear, but some basics will make your tours safer and more enjoyable.

Helmet. Absolutely essential for your safety. Make sure you wear one that fits properly with a secure strap. You should wear it so the front of the helmet comes almost to your eyebrows, to really protect your brain if you have an accident.

A bike that fits. Make sure you and any companions are riding the right size bike and that your seat is positioned properly. If the seat is too low, your legs will tire too quickly; if it sits too high, you might injure your knees. You'll also have difficulty handling the bike properly in either case.

Checking out your bike. Check your tire pressure, brakes, handlebars, cables, and reflectors before you start riding to make sure that everything works properly before you get 10 miles out into the country.

Water. This liquid is a must any time of year but particularly in the hot, humid summer months. Always drink before you're thirsty and consume at least a pint of water every hour. Bike shops carry water bottles and holders that can attach to your bike frame.

Bike lock. A strong lock is essential if you plan to leave your bike for sight-seeing or other stops. It's important to secure both wheels and the frame to an immovable object.

Clothing. You can wear just about anything to ride a bike as long as it won't get caught in the chain or other bike parts and throw you off the bike. For longer rides, however, padded cycling shorts or tights prevent chafing and won't bunch up while you ride. Jerseys and jackets of lightweight materials that wick water away from your skin are especially helpful when you ride in colder weather. Padded gloves also protect your hands from numbness or scrapes if you should fall.

Bike computer. These neat gizmos that clip to your handlebars will help you determine mileage and help keep you on track with the directions. They're available in bike shops and by mail order.

Cellular phone or repair kit. If you do run into problems, a lightweight cellular phone in your bike bag can be a big help. (Of course you'll need numbers with you so you'll know whom to call.) If you don't have a cellular phone, I'd suggest carrying a small repair kit or at least a spare tube, tire irons, and a frame pump.

Bike bags. Speaking of carrying things, you'll also need a small seat bag—ideal for tools and pocket change. A handlebar bag with a clear pocket on top is handy for keeping your map and directions right in front of you as you ride.

Glasses or sunglasses. Good eye protection can be important to keep bugs and other debris out of your eyes while you're riding. Preventing harm from ultraviolet rays is a consideration, too, especially if you'll be riding for several hours.

Riding Safely

A bike is a vehicle. In North Carolina, as in many other states, bicycles are considered vehicles and must obey the same rules of the road. That means cyclists have the same rights but also the same responsibilities when sharing the road with motor vehicles. Even if you're right, however, that doesn't mean you'll win if you tangle with a two-ton car. So courtesy and prudently giving way to others is your safest bet.

Many of North Carolina's secondary roadways are designated as either local or state bike routes. These bike route signs help alert motorists to the presence of cyclists. North Carolina was also the first state to develop a SHARE THE ROAD caution sign with a small bicycle emblem under it. You're likely to see these on highways with more motorized traffic.

As a vehicle you're entitled to a lane, but be considerate of motorists behind you. In North Carolina cyclists may ride two abreast, but groups usually move to single file out of courtesy when motorists are trying to pass. Remember the Golden Rule!

The roadway. These routes have been selected because they usually have less traffic than alternatives do, but conditions change. It's up to you to be alert for potholes, debris on the road, construction projects, and other road hazards. Especially in the summer months, you might want to call ahead to find out about road construction and conditions before starting your ride.

Look around you. Always be conscious of your surroundings, particularly if you're riding alone. I've done a lot of cycling by myself and use my rearview mirror and checking ahead to anticipate problem situations or conditions. Consider carrying a cellular phone or riding with a friend or a group.

Be visible. One reason for brightly patterned clothing for cyclists is to make us stand out in traffic. Especially in town, myriad signs and other traffic can distract drivers. So wear bright colors, contrasting colors to make you visible. While I don't recommend riding at night, if you choose to do so, you should wear reflective clothing and equip your bike with a bright front light and effective red rear reflector. Some cyclists place a flashing strobe on the back of the bike to alert drivers.

Cyclists can be really hard to see in the very early morning and late evening hours, when shadows and the angle of the sun can keep drivers from seeing us. Take special care at these times. At all times remember that drivers are looking for other vehicles, so act like one. If you need to do so for safety, ride farther out into the lane so you're more visible for drivers. This strategy is especially advisable on the few sections of these routes where there are four lanes. Always signal your intention to turn or change lanes so that drivers can react properly.

More Bicycle Information

Division of Bicycle and Pedestrian Transportation
North Carolina Department of Transportation
P.O. Box 25201
Raleigh, NC 27611
(919) 733–2804

Touring Information
League of American Bicyclists
190 West Ostend Street, Suite 120
Baltimore, MD 21230
(410) 539–3399

Neither The Globe Pequot Press nor the author assume liability for accidents happening to, or injuries substained by, readers who engage in the activities described in this book.

Rolling on the River
Fleetwood to Todd in Ashe County

Number of miles:	20.5
Approximate pedaling time:	2 hours
Terrain:	Flat
Traffic:	Slow, friendly
Things to see:	South Fork of the New River, Todd General Store, Christmas tree farms, fresco in church in nearby West Jefferson
Food:	Snacks at general store in Todd, at stores and restaurants in West Jefferson, and at intersection of U.S. 421 and U.S. 221

This wonderfully easy ride, long popular with North Carolina cyclists, covers a stretch of road that used to be the route for the railroad up to Abingdon, Virginia. Established well before most rail-to-trails conversions, this route connects two small farming communities in Ashe County in the northwesternmost corner of North Carolina. Although motor vehicles must use the very narrow road, most drivers are friendly sorts who wave as they pass.

The road hugs the south fork of the New River most of the route as it wends its way through these mountain valleys. Most people are amazed to find that they can ride a mountain route that is so flat, "it's downhill both ways," as the local saying about the route goes. In warm weather tubing and canoeing bring many people to the river. The cool, shallow waters flow briskly enough to keep canoes moving while slowly enough that those in the canoes can enjoy the scenery and wave to the many cyclists on their bikes.

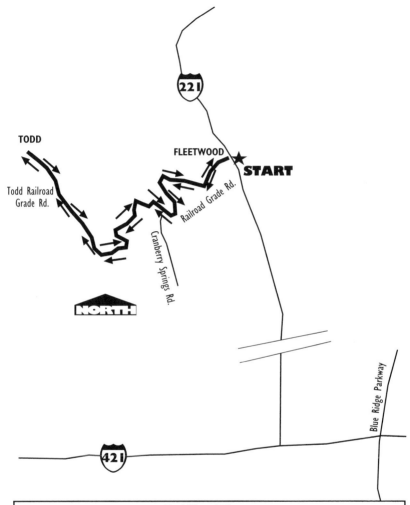

TODD

Todd Railroad
Grade Rd.

FLEETWOOD

★ START

Railroad Grade Rd.

Cranberry Springs Rd.

NORTH

221

421

Blue Ridge Parkway

Getting There

From U.S. 421, turn north onto U.S. 221. Drive 6.1 miles north on U.S. 221, and then make a sharp left turn on Railroad Grade Road in Fleetwood. (There's a sign to the Fleetwood Post Office.) Road descends to river level along a very curvy stretch and then straightens and flattens as you enter the town of Fleetwood. Public parking in grassy area across from church and post office.

DIREC-TIONS at a glance

0.0 From parking area across the street from church and post office on Railroad Grade Road, turn left onto Railroad Grade Road.

3.51 Bear right on Railroad Grade Road. (New River Bridge Road [SR 1105] goes off to the left.)

5.22 Bear right on Railroad Grade Road. (Brown Road [SR 1104] goes off to the left.)

6.39 Bear right on Railroad Grade Road. (Cranberry Springs Road [SR 1100] goes off to the left.) *Note*: Railroad Grade Road becomes Todd Railroad Grade Road (SR 1100) at this intersection.

10.25 Arrive in Todd at Todd General Store. Turn around and retrace route.

20.5 Return to Fleetwood.

The quiet of this pastoral setting is good for whatever may trouble your mind. In some places thickets of rhododendron on steep hillsides dip their branches into quickly flowing streams that feed the river. These sections must have inspired those who lobbied diligently in the 1970s for the New to be declared a National Wild and Scenic River.

Lush green pastures color the roadsides in the sparsely populated areas. Sometimes goats and sheep graze. In others the more familiar cows and horses share space. On one visit to the area, I came upon a woodchuck munching vegetation by the side of the road and was able to get within 3 feet of it before it scurried into the underbrush.

While Ashe County is home to several major businesses, most of the residents rely on farming or tourism for their livelihoods. Some rolling hills along the river sprout with young pines and spruces destined for Christmas tree markets all over the East Coast.

Other sights to see in the area include two contemporary religious frescoes. One graces Holy Trinity Church in Glendale Springs while the other is located in St. Mary's Church on Beaver Creek School Road in West Jefferson.

The mineral springs in the area used to attract people who wanted to benefit from their healing qualities. Shatley Springs in northern Ashe County is noted for its Southern country cooking, served up family style, but leave your calorie and cholesterol counter behind if you go there.

At the Todd General Store, you can see products from the 1930s and 1940s that have long since disappeared from today's supermarket shelves. The store is also a museum of sorts, with old farm implements and advertising signs. A few provisions, homemade goodies, and a variety of cold drinks are available for sale. You might just want to sip your drink while resting on a bench on the front porch overlooking the New River before heading back to Fleetwood.

"Valley of the Cross" Tour:
Valle Crucis

Number of miles:	30.5
Approximate pedaling time:	3 hours
Terrain:	Hilly and rolling
Traffic:	Light except on U.S. 421
Things to see:	Mast General Store, Mast Inn, rugged mountain roads, rhododendrons, Christmas tree farms
Food:	At Mast General Store

The Mast General Store will certainly take you back in time. Set up like the old country store it has been for about a century, its shelves carry cast-iron pots and frying pans along with the latest in hiking shoes and Birkenstocks. The renewed popularity of the store in the last decade or so encouraged the newer owners to establish the Mast Inn up the hill from the store as well as a second location in Boone.

From the store this tour loops through the mountain countryside past farms and small communities. Mast Gap Road at 1.3 miles begins a fairly steep climb but takes you past dense hardwood forests, acres of Christmas trees in neatly trimmed rows, small white churches, and masses of rhododendrons. The route follows part of the Watauga River Valley through small mountain crests and lush green valleys.

After you turn right on Old U.S. 421 (at 3.5 miles), you'll see a swiftly running stream and mounds of rocks. It's no surprise, then, that many of the homes and businesses in the area are built of native stone. At 4.5 miles Dale Adams Road takes you through Henson Hollar—a misspelling of the Southern Appalachian word *holler*. Regional pronunciation dictates that words ending in *ow*

are pronounced like *er,* so *holler* means a hollow or small valley between two mountains. The road climbs gradually through Henson Hollar.

Laurel Branch Road (starting at 7.0 miles) is a narrow paved road, somewhat uneven with no shoulders, but there's very little traffic in this area. You'll find most people friendly to cyclists; it doesn't hurt to raise your hand in greeting, either, if they don't beat you to it. This stretch takes you almost to the Tennessee border.

After you turn right on U.S. 421 (at 11.7 miles), watch for heavier traffic and a steep climb. Fortunately an extra right climbing lane provides a greater margin of safety. Slabtown Road (SR 1302) is the first paved road to the right. Be on the lookout because you come up on it suddenly and it begins with a sharp turn. The name changes to Mabel School Road. You'll probably wonder how the residents on this very curvy road manage in the winter when the area typically receives about 58 inches of snow!

The return trip along Mast Gap Road (at 27.1 miles) offers great views of the valley and rustic log houses with stone fireplaces. This road leads you back to NC–194 and the Mast General Store.

This ride takes place in Avery County, which was named after Colonel Waighstill Avery. The colonel served in the Revolutionary War from 1779 until 1781 and later became the first attorney general of North Carolina. All the county's approximately 15,000 residents live above 3,000 feet in elevation. The highest ski slopes in the South, golf resorts, and Grandfather Mountain attract visitors to the area year-round, making tourism the leading industry in this rural county. The second largest industry is Christmas tree and ornamental shrubbery farming, giving the county its nickname of Fraser Fir Capital of the World.

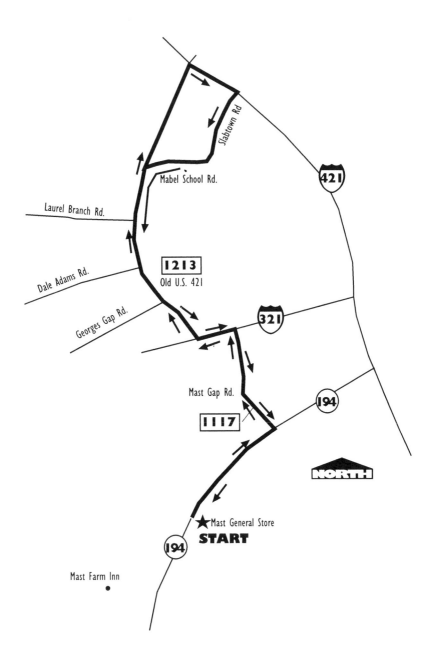

421

Slabtown Rd

Mabel School Rd.

Laurel Branch Rd.

Dale Adams Rd.

1213
Old U.S. 421

Georges Gap Rd.

321

194

Mast Gap Rd.

1117

NORTH

194

★ Mast General Store
START

Mast Farm Inn
●

DIREC-TIONS at a glance

0.0 From Mast General Store in Valle Crucis, turn right out of public parking lot behind store onto NC–194.

0.6 Cross bridge.

1.3 Turn left onto Mast Gap Road (SR 1117).

3.4 Turn left onto U.S. 321.

3.5 Turn right onto Old U.S. 421 (SR 1213).

4.5 Continue straight past Dale Adams Road through Henson Hollar.

11.7 Turn right onto U.S. 421 (near Tennessee state line).

18.5 Turn right onto Slabtown Road (SR 1302), first road to right.

20.8 Turn left onto Old U.S. 421 (SR 1213).

26.8 Turn left onto U.S. 321.

27.1 Turn right onto Mast Gap Road (SR 1117).

29.3 Turn right onto NC–194.

30.5 Turn left into parking lot at Mast General Store.

Getting There

From Winston-Salem, take U.S. 421 west to Boone. Turn south onto NC–194 to Valle Crucis and Mast General Store. There's a large parking area behind the store.

Sailing on the
Linn Cove Viaduct
Blue Ridge Parkway

Number of miles:	29.4
Approximate pedaling time:	4 hours
Terrain:	Mountainous; although the climbs are gradual, many are long
Traffic:	Can be heavy in the fall and around holidays, but no trucks, and speed is limited to 45 miles per hour
Things to see:	Wonderful mountain vistas, Julian Price Lake, Moses Cone Manor House and Craft Center, Linn Cove Viaduct, Linn Cove Information Center
Food:	No places to buy food along this stretch of the parkway; restrooms at Manor House, picnic area, and Linn Cove Information Center

This ride begins with a long, gradual climb, about 7 miles in length. Fortunately, there are plenty of overlooks and spectacular views along the way to break up the climb. Of course the reward is a glorious 7-mile downhill run at the end of the ride that makes the climb well worth it. Plan to take advantage of all the overlooks along the way and enjoy the variety of mountain scenery. During late June and early July the rhododendrons, with their large white and pink blooms, can be spectacularly showy.

The Blue Ridge Parkway that runs through Virginia and North Carolina is a huge monument to the heroic efforts of the Civilian Conservation Corps, which built much of the parkway

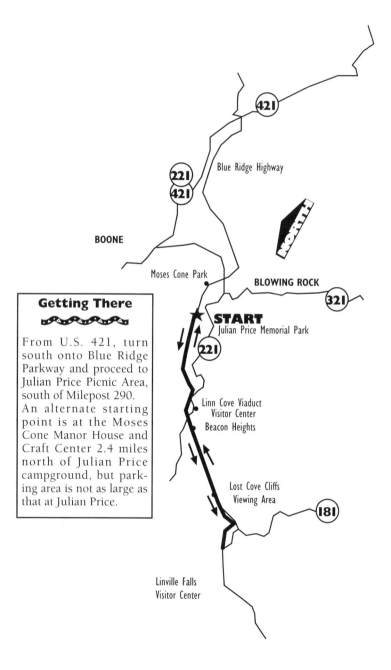

421

Blue Ridge Highway

221
421

NORTH

BOONE

Moses Cone Park

BLOWING ROCK

321

Getting There

START
Julian Price Memorial Park

221

From U.S. 421, turn south onto Blue Ridge Parkway and proceed to Julian Price Picnic Area, south of Milepost 290. An alternate starting point is at the Moses Cone Manor House and Craft Center 2.4 miles north of Julian Price campground, but parking area is not as large as that at Julian Price.

Linn Cove Viaduct
Visitor Center
Beacon Heights

Lost Cove Cliffs
Viewing Area

181

Linville Falls
Visitor Center

DIREC-TIONS at a glance

0.0 From parking area at Julian Price Picnic Area, turn right onto the Blue Ridge Parkway, going south.

2.1 Intersection.

2.6 Overlook.

3.4 View Calloway Peak of Grandfather Mountain.

3.7 Cross Bone Fork.

4.1 Cross Green Mountain Creek.

4.4 Green Mountain Overlook.

5.7 Pilot Ridge Overlook.

6.1 Overlook.

6.8 Rough Ridge Overlook.

7.6 Cross Wilson Creek.

7.7 Wilson Creek Overlook.

8.1 Yonahlassee Overlook.

8.2 Linn Cove Viaduct.

8.7 Linn Cove Information Center.

8.9 Stack Rock Creek.

9.1 Stack Rock Parking Area.

9.5 Pass U.S. 221 exit to Linville and Grandfather Mountain.

9.7 Beacon Heights Parking Area.

11.0 Grandfather Mountain Parking Overlook.

11.9 Grandfather Mountain Parking Area.

12.5 Pass intersection with SR 1151.

12.7 Trailhead for Flat Rock Trail and beginning of Pisgah National Forest.

14.5 Lost Cove Cliffs Viewing Area. Turn around and retrace route north up Blue Ridge Parkway.

29.4 Arrive at Julian Price Picnic Area.

on the crest of the Blue Ridge during the 1930s. This tour includes the newest section, the Linn Cove Viaduct, which was completed in 1987.

Begun in 1935 at Cumberland Knob in North Carolina, 462.5 miles of the parkway had been completed by 1967. The last stretch, though, posed one of the greatest challenges: how to build a road at an elevation of 4,100 feet without damaging one of the world's oldest mountains. The resulting Linn Cove Viaduct has been called "the most complicated concrete bridge ever built, snaking around the boulder-strewn Linn Cove in a sweeping 'S' curve." The viaduct is 1,243 feet long and contains 153 segments weighing 50 tons each.

The overlook at 6.1 miles gives a splendid view of the sheer granite cliffs on top of the mountain. Along much of the parkway carefully crafted stone walls and zigzag split-rail fences—in some cases double split-rail—define the parkway's boundaries. Because there is no truck traffic allowed on the parkway and the roadway is not scraped in the winter, the pavement remains quite smooth and great for cycling. In most places grassy shoulders grace the sides of the road.

While the viaduct and the spectacular views from the parkway are the key attractions on this tour, a few human-built places are also interesting to visit. The Moses Cone Manor House on this stretch of the parkway was constructed at the turn of the century by textile magnate Moses H. Cone. He and his wife built this elegant twenty-room manor house on Flat Top Mountain, which afforded them wonderful views of the mountains' natural beauty.

Across the 3,500 acres Cone purchased spread glorious groves of rhododendrons, mountain laurels, and wild azaleas broken only by ridgetop meadows setting the stage for the magnificence of Grandfather Mountain's rocky crest. The 25 miles of trails crisscrossing the property invite horseback riders in summer and cross-country skiers in winter to enjoy the natural setting so appreciated and conserved by the Cones.

The manor house is now home to the Parkway Craft Center,

which showcases the work of members of the Southern Highland Craft Guild, recognized for excellence in artisanship and design. Artistic skills that have passed through several generations are preserved in the lovely pottery, baskets, ironwork, hand-carved wood, and many other distinctive crafts. There is no charge to visit the galleries because almost every craft item is available for purchase.

The turnaround point at Lost Cove Cliffs—elevation 3,500 feet—is the best vantage point for the Brown Mountain Lights of folklore. The lights are first mentioned in American Indian lore in the early 1700s and have continued to puzzle observers for centuries. In 1913 the U.S. Geological Survey studied the lights and concluded that they were headlights of locomotives in the valley, yet after a flood a few years later stopped the trains, the lights continued to appear. Another study in 1922 speculated that the lights from a variety of sources such as autos, towns, and brush fires were refracted and bent skyward by the unstable air currents in the valleys. Phosphorus, UFOs, radium ore deposits, and marsh gas have been put forth as other possible causes of the mysterious lights.

Julian Price Memorial Park, the starting point and terminus for this tour, began as a retreat for an insurance executive and now offers a large lake, campground, picnic area, and short trails for hiking. It's located between Mileposts 295.1 and 298, a great place to begin and end your adventure on the Blue Ridge Parkway.

Yancey River Ramble:
Burnsville

Number of miles:	37.7 (20.0 for shorter loop)
Approximate pedaling time:	4½ hours
Terrain:	Rolling
Traffic:	Very light on secondary roads to heavy on major highways
Things to see:	Beautiful mountain scenery, streams and rivers; old tobacco barns, footbridges across the rivers to houses; country churches and communities
Food:	Several stores and restaurants along U.S. 19E toward Burnsville but very little along the route

Imagine being in the midst of the Blue Ridge Mountains, following streams and rivers with only a couple of minor hills to climb. That's what this route is like. With every turn you follow a stream that then feeds into a river, so that you're always next to water. Burnsville itself feels like a step back in time. This feeling continues as you ride this route where not much has changed over the last fifty years.

The first part of the route takes you along a curvy, narrow road through mountain valleys filled with tobacco or corn fields. You'll pass the tin-roofed Jack's Creek Presbyterian Church and, in summer, see large round hay bales dotting fields, a sure sign that you're near dairy or cattle farms.

At 4.6 miles Coxes Creek Road goes off to the left and you'll see Jack's Creek on the right. Steep mountain pastures climb from roadside to summits perhaps 1,000 feet above. Over the next 4 miles, Jack's Creek gurgles beside the road, creating a moist envi-

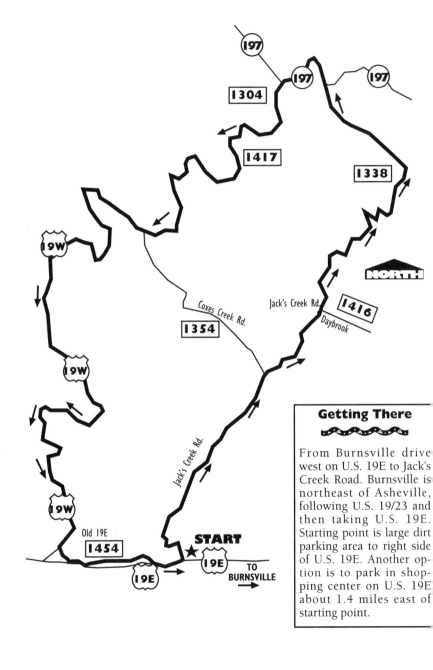

197

1304

197

197

1417

1338

19W

1354

Coxes Creek Rd.

Jack's Creek Rd. **1416**

Daybrook

NORTH

19W

Jack's Creek Rd.

19W

19W

Old 19E **1454**

START ★

19E

19E

TO BURNSVILLE

Getting There

From Burnsville drive west on U.S. 19E to Jack's Creek Road. Burnsville is northeast of Asheville, following U.S. 19/23 and then taking U.S. 19E. Starting point is large dirt parking area to right side of U.S. 19E. Another option is to park in shopping center on U.S. 19E about 1.4 miles east of starting point.

DIRECTIONS at a glance

37.7 miles

0.0 From the east on U.S. 19E, turn right onto Jack's Creek Road (SR 1336).

4.6 Pass Coxes Creek Road on left.

6.6 Stay on Jack's Creek Road. Jack's Creek is on right side of road. Clearmont School is to right on SR 1416.

9.4 Sign on left for North Bend Church.

10.2 Turn left onto SR 1338. Jack's Creek flows into Toe River on right.

13.3 Cross one-lane bridge over Toe River.

13.4 *Caution:* railroad tracks. Cross them and then veer left, staying on SR 1338. (A gravel road goes off to right.)

13.6 Turn left onto NC–197.

15.1 NC–197 goes off to right, but stay straight on what becomes SR 1304.

16.5 Turn left onto SR 1417 after crossing one-lane bridge over Toe River.

20.2 Turn left onto U.S. 19W South at stop sign.

21.9 Coxes Creek Road joins U.S. 19W.

26.6 Turn left onto U.S. 19W South at yield sign.

27.9 Cross bridge over Cane River.

30.1 Cross another bridge over Cane River.

35.0 Turn left onto Old U.S. 19E (SR 1454). (U.S. 19W goes off to right.)

37.1 Turn left onto U.S. 19E.

37.7 Arrive at Jack's Creek Road.

20.0 miles

Follow directions for longer loop until 4.6 miles.

4.6 Turn left onto Coxes Creek Road, which comes into U.S. 19W near Ramseyton. Follow directions for longer loop starting at 21.9 miles.

ronment for the profusion of wildflowers on the roadside.

At 10.2 miles Jack's Creek flows into the Toe River. I speculate that the river got its name because it's so shallow it barely wets your toes. The clear, cold water looks inviting on a hot summer's day. The one-lane bridge at 13.3 miles recalls earlier times when horse-drawn wagons crossed the river at this point. Take care when crossing because the sight distances on either side of the bridge are not good and the bridge is so narrow that's there not sufficient room for a car to pass while a cyclist is on the bridge.

At 13.6 miles you turn left on NC–197, with the railroad tracks up the bank to the right. Although rail usage has continued to decline, the tracks serve as a reminder of how important the railroad was to connecting these remote areas to the rest of North Carolina and the world. The railroad, too, liked to follow rivers and streams when laying tracks because the banks are generally flatter.

At 15.1 miles our route continues straight as the road becomes SR 1304. NC–197 bears off to the right and across the railroad tracks. The Huntdale community is situated at 16.3 miles.

Along U.S. 19W it's surprising to see the large number of footbridges across the Cane River to the houses on the other bank of the river. In some cases the owners' pickup trucks or cars are parked next to the road. But in other cases the vehicles are mysteriously parked next to the houses, yet there's no sign of a road for entrance or egress. All manner of signs warn that crossing these bridges is at your own risk. Be sure to check out all the different types of construction and decide if you'd be willing to cross.

At 27.9 and 30.1 miles, bridges cross the Cane River, which bends and winds its way around the mountains. At 35.0 miles you'll turn left on U.S. 19E, which may have heavy traffic, including trucks. At this intersection U.S. 19W goes off to the right. The speed limit along U.S. 19E is 55 miles per hour, so it's quite a change from the laid-back rural roads to this point. Fortunately this stretch is not very long, and you're soon back to the starting point at the intersection with Jack's Creek Road.

The Road to Biltmore:
Asheville

Number of miles:	20
Approximate pedaling time:	4 hours
Terrain:	Hilly
Traffic:	Busy along some major streets but light on side streets
Things to see:	Biltmore House and Estate, Biltmore Village, Grove Park Inn, Pack Square, downtown Asheville, Thomas Wolfe Memorial, mountains around Asheville
Food:	All along the route

Cycling in Asheville is not for the fainthearted, but the rewards are well worth the effort because the city is surrounded by the beautiful Great Smoky Mountains and the Blue Ridge Mountains with a few mountains in the middle for good measure.

It's easy to see why Asheville is one of the most popular mountain resort areas in the eastern United States. The Blue Ridge Parkway skirts its perimeter, and two rivers—the Swannanoa and the French Broad—divide it. No wonder George Washington Vanderbilt chose this area in the late nineteenth century as the site of his fabulous estate.

This tour begins in the southern part of Asheville in a premier residential area known as Biltmore Forest because it abuts the Biltmore Estate. The route passes the entrance to the Biltmore Estate at 4.7 miles. Self-guided tours of the estate include the upstairs and downstairs of the mansion itself, the gardens, the greenhouse, and the Biltmore Estate Winery, which offers

tastings as well. You should allow a minimum of four hours to take the complete tour.

The mansion, built using distinctive architectural features from famous French châteaux, contains 250 rooms. Not all the rooms are open, but the main living areas upstairs give a feel for the posh life the Vanderbilts enjoyed. The downstairs has the less formal rooms, including kitchen, work areas, and servant quarters. New rooms are opened periodically, and major artworks from the collection are on display throughout the house.

The gardens surrounding the house are comprised of seventy-five acres of formal gardens and grounds designed by Frederick Law Olmsted, who designed Central Park in New York City. Across U.S. 25 from the estate is Biltmore Village, an interesting assortment of craft shops and upscale boutiques with many restaurants in the area. From this point the route climbs a half-mile hill toward downtown. Fortunately the right lane widens about halfway up the hill to give cars more room to pass heavily breathing cyclists.

At 6.9 miles is Pack Place, Asheville's arts, education, and science center. The complex combines performance and exhibit spaces with retail shops, bringing arts, science, culture, and entertainment together in one location. The Asheville Art Museum is located here, along with the Colburn Gem and Mineral Museum.

When you turn left on Market Street, you'll find yourself on cobblestones for about 1 block through one of Asheville's restaurant districts. Then at 7.25 miles you'll see the Thomas Wolfe Memorial in a large white house that was the author's boyhood home. The house was clearly the model for the boardinghouse in Wolfe's famous novel, *Look Homeward, Angel*. Tours of the house take about thirty minutes.

The next point of interest is the Grove Park Inn at the top of Macon Avenue. The short, steady climb starting at 8.2 miles passes through a residential area with lovely old homes. The Grove Park, one of the South's grand old resorts, was built in 1913 on the hillside overlooking downtown Asheville and the surrounding mountains. The inn's remarkable architecture rep-

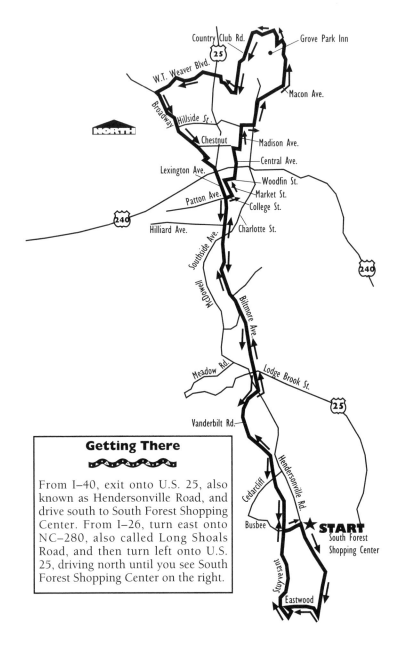

Country Club Rd.
Grove Park Inn
25
W.T. Weaver Blvd.
Macon Ave.
Broadway
Hillside St.
NORTH
Chestnut
Madison Ave.
Central Ave.
Lexington Ave.
Woodfin St.
Market St.
Patton Ave.
College St.
240
Hilliard Ave.
Charlotte St.
Southside Ave.
McDowell
Biltmore Ave.
240
Meadow Rd.
Lodge Brook St.
25
Vanderbilt Rd.
Cedarcliff
Hendersonville Rd.
Busbee
★ START
South Forest
Shopping Center
Stuyvesant
Eastwood

Getting There

From I–40, exit onto U.S. 25, also known as Hendersonville Road, and drive south to South Forest Shopping Center. From I–26, turn east onto NC–280, also called Long Shoals Road, and then turn left onto U.S. 25, driving north until you see South Forest Shopping Center on the right.

DIREC-TIONS at a glance

0.0 From parking lot on U.S. 25 south of downtown Asheville at South Forest Shopping Center, at stoplight where shopping entrance intersects U.S. 25, turn left onto U.S. 25, also called Hendersonville Road.

1.4 Turn right onto Eastwood Drive.

1.9 Turn right onto Stuyvesant Road.

2.8 Cross intersection with Cedarcliff, at which point Stuyvesant becomes Vanderbilt Road.

4.7 Turn left onto Hendersonville Road, which becomes Biltmore Avenue. Entrance to Biltmore Estate is here; you may stop for a tour.

6.9 Turn right onto College Street at Pack Square downtown (street name changes to Patton to the left).

7.0 Turn left onto Market Street.

7.2 Turn right onto Woodfin Street.

7.25 Pass or stop for a tour at Thomas Wolfe Memorial on right.

7.3 Turn left onto Central Avenue.

7.6 Turn right onto East Chestnut Street at stop sign, then make an immediate left onto Madison Avenue.

7.9 Turn right onto Hillside Street.

8.0 Turn left onto Charlotte Street.

8.2 Turn right onto Macon Avenue at Grove Park Inn sign.

9.0 Turn left into Grove Park Inn. Bear left at first stop sign, then turn right just in front of inn and continue to bear right through parking lot.

9.2 Turn left at second stop sign.

9.3 Turn right into Grove Park Homespun Shops (allow 0.2 mile to circle the drive).

9.5 Turn right back onto the main drive through Grove Park property.

9.8 Turn left onto Country Club Road.

10.1 Turn left onto Kimberly Avenue.

10.4 Turn right onto Evelyn Place, then right onto Murdock Avenue.

10.7 At stop sign bear left on Murdock Avenue to stoplight at Merrimon, and then turn left onto Merrimon Avenue and immediately right onto W.T. Weaver Boulevard at next light.

11.2 Possible side trip through campus of University of North Carolina at Asheville.

11.9 Turn left onto Broadway Street into downtown Asheville.

13.0 Go straight under I–240.

14.2 At intersection with Hiawassee, continue straight on Broadway Street, although its name changes to Lexington Street

15.9 Turn left onto Hilliard Avenue, then right onto Biltmore Avenue.

17.8 Turn right onto Vanderbilt Road at stoplight.

19.7 Turn left onto Busbee Road, then bear left at next fork so that you come out at traffic signal.

19.9 Continue straight across U.S. 25 (Hendersonville Road) into South Forest Shopping Center parking lot.

---

resents an outstanding engineering feat because of the massive granite boulders used in construction.

As you pass around the side of the inn, you'll see the Homespun Shops, Grovewood Gallery, and museums on your right. The Homespun Museum contains implements from a bygone era and is next to the Antique Car Museum. A flute maker, glassblower, weaver, and other artisans share studio space in the building.

At 11.2 miles is the entrance to the University of North Carolina at Asheville, which could be the starting point for an optional side tour. Immediately past the university entrance are the Botanical Gardens, providing ten acres of native plants.

After you turn back onto Biltmore Avenue, you'll see St. Joseph's Medical Center and signs for the Smith-McDowell House, another option for a short but hilly side trip. The route concludes with a serene ride past the elegant homes of Biltmore Forest.

Tour de Cashiers

Number of miles:	10.5
Approximate pedaling time:	1½ hours
Terrain:	Mountainous
Traffic:	Light on back roads to moderate along U.S. 64
Things to see:	Mountains, gorgeous stands of rhododendrons, mountain streams, small homesteads, true mountain roads
Food:	Restaurants and convenience stores in Cashiers

This short, scenic route is deceptively difficult because of the terrain and the hairpin curves, but if you're up for a quick—but strenuous—ride in the mountains, this is a great place!

Cashiers, located in the southern crest of the Blue Ridge of the Appalachian mountain chain, is situated on a plateau surrounded by the Nantahala National Forest. European immigrants from the British Isles were attracted to this area in the early 1800s by the mountains and the wild beauty. By the end of the century, the area had become a popular summering place for the South's elite families. A quick glance at the variety of license plates from different states attests to Cashiers's continuing popularity as a summer resort.

Cashiers's location on the Eastern Continental Divide at 3,487 feet, combined with the number of rivers flowing through the area, gives it many natural wonders at which to marvel. It's easy to see why people continue to vacation and live here. It has tall mountain peaks, deep valleys, many waterfalls, lush forests and mountain plants, and a serene setting. The tallest mountains

surrounding Cashiers soar to around 5,000 feet, pushing gigantic boulders toward the sky. Whiteside Mountain along U.S. 64 West boasts the highest sheer cliffs in the eastern United States at 4,930 feet. A rock climber's dream, these cliffs are closed to climbers during the nesting season of the peregrine falcon in the spring.

Cashiers is not the place to go if you want lots of noise and a busy nightlife. Rather, you should come for a renewed appreciation of nature and the powerful forces that have shaped this area. Just a few miles down NC–107 lies the point where North Carolina, South Carolina, and Georgia come together. Most people don't realize that Georgia and North Carolina share a rather significant common border. From the tall peaks south of Cashiers, you can look into three states.

Jackson County, in which Cashiers is located, is within what once were Cherokee Indian lands. In the late eighteenth century, Cherokees from other parts of the state pushed westward to join those already living in what is now Jackson County. The establishment of the Foster trading station drew more white colonial and European settlers to the area. The station was set up on the white people's land but at the boundary so that Indians could trade there, too.

By the mid-nineteenth century, thriving communities were scattered throughout the area. When it was determined that a new county was to be formed in this area, the inhabitants were divided in their loyalties to two notable American heroes—Daniel Webster, a great orator, and Andrew Jackson, a popular hero and founder of Jacksonian democracy. They decided to name the county after Jackson and the county seat after Webster, thus appeasing all parties. The official ceremony took place at the log cabin erected by pioneer Daniel Bryson in 1853.

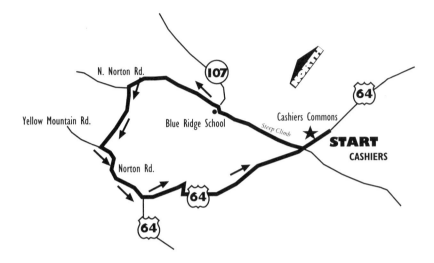

N. Norton Rd.

107

Yellow Mountain Rd.

Blue Ridge School

Cashiers Commons

Steep Climb

★ **START**

64

CASHIERS

Norton Rd.

64

64

Getting There

From U.S. 64 in Cashiers, turn north onto NC–107 and into the parking lot at Cashiers Commons, about 0.2 mile north of the intersection of U.S. 64 and NC–107.

DIRECTIONS at a glance

0.0	From parking lot at Cashiers Commons about 0.2 mile north of U.S. 64, turn right onto NC–107.
1.6	Turn left onto North Norton Road. (NC–107 goes off to right.)
3.5	Turn left onto Norton Road.

5.0   Turn left to stay on Norton. (Yellow Mountain Road goes off to right.)

7.1   Turn left onto U.S. 64 East.

10.3   Turn left onto NC–107.

10.5   Turn right into Cashiers Commons.

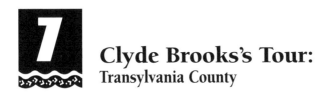

Clyde Brooks's Tour:
Transylvania County

Number of miles:	39.0
Approximate pedaling time:	3 hours
Terrain:	Rolling, with a few moderate climbs
Traffic:	Light except along U.S. 64/276
Things to see:	River valley, surrounding mountains, beautiful farms and forests, wildflowers, Brevard College
Food:	Service station at corner of Crab Creek Road and U.S. 64 and in restaurants and grocery stores in Brevard

This tour takes its name from a resident of Brevard and Transylvania County who suggested this route, which turned out to be quite lovely. Transylvania County was formed from parts of Henderson and Jackson counties on May 20, 1861. The first planned order of business was to build a two-story brick courthouse and jail. North Carolina had just voted that very day to secede from the Union, however, so the tax monies the new county collected had to be used to send local recruits to the Civil War.

At that time, the area was inhabited by indigenous Indians and by white settlers who from the late 1700s onward had been attracted to the area by the mild climate, rich soil, abundant wildlife and game, and beautiful setting. This route demonstrates the attractiveness of the area and why settlers and tourists have been drawn here since the earliest European settlements were established.

There's a bit of traffic to contend with at the beginning and very end. U.S. 64/276 is a divided, four-lane highway but not fully controlled access, so cyclists can use it. Fortunately, the lanes are wide and the distance along this road is not great. Once you turn onto U.S. 64, the road is a two-lane highway, again with wide lanes and a smooth road surface.

At 6.7 miles you leave the traffic, turning onto Crab Creek Road (SR 1528) for a more rural and peaceful setting. Along Talley Road (SR 1527), onto which you turned from Crab Creek Road, the road flirts with the French Broad River while Queen Anne's lace, daylilies, dandelions, and wild sweet peas grace the roadside. The river supposedly got its name from Frenchman Jean Couture in 1696. He was a follower of explorer Robert Cavalier LaSalle. The river is noted for its complexity, with four major forks: the North Fork, the West Fork, the East Fork, and the Middle Fork. Its valley through the Brevard area is considered one of the most beautiful river valleys in North Carolina, draining approximately 2,800 square miles of mountains and valleys.

You'll see little traffic on this flat-to-rolling route as you pass a tree nursery and dairy farm and negotiate the sharp curves necessitated by the whims of the river. For some mysterious reason, Talley Road's name changes to Pleasant Grove Road somewhere around 3.1 miles after you turned onto it. Then 1.4 miles later Pleasant Grove Road goes off to the right. At a later point its name changes again to River Road (SR 1191). From 13.4 to 13.8 miles the pavement is interrupted by this short stretch of rough, packed gravel.

After you turn onto Big Willow Road, broad bands of corn dress the shoulders of the river in summer. At 16.1 miles an apple orchard provides a temptation to summer cyclists. After you turn again onto Crab Creek Road, you'll be treated in summer to trees shading the road, the shade broken only by clumps of bright daylilies and pale pink rhododendron flowers.

A long hill brings you past small lakes and camps, then Holmes Educational State Forest, before you head back toward Brevard and the starting point at Brevard College. Established formally in 1934, Brevard College's roots date to 1853. During those many years, the college at one time or another offered high school, seminary, two- and four-year college programs, and

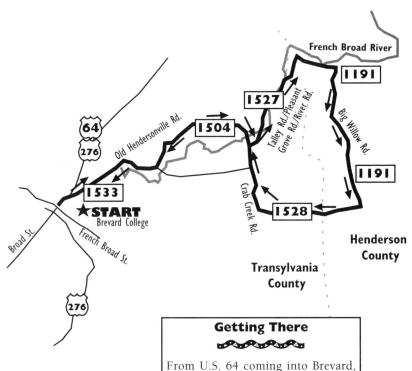

French Broad River

1191

64
276

Old Hendersonville Rd.

1527

Talley Rd./Pleasant Grove Rd./River Rd.

Big Willow Rd.

1504

1191

1533

★**START**
Brevard College

Crab Creek Rd.

1528

Broad St.

French Broad St.

276

Henderson County

Transylvania County

Getting There

From U.S. 64 coming into Brevard, head west toward Brevard College downtown on Broad Street (U.S. 64/276). Shopping center parking lot is at intersection of Broad and French Broad Streets across from college.

0.0 From traffic signal by parking lot at intersection of Broad Street (U.S. 64/276) and French Broad Street in downtown Brevard, across from Brevard College, turn right onto Broad Street (U.S. 64/276).

0.6 Bear right onto Old Hendersonville Road (SR 1533). (U.S. 64/276 goes off to left.)

2.4 Cross bridge over French Broad River.

3.3 Bear left onto Old Hendersonville Road (SR 1504).

6.4 Turn right onto Crab Creek Road (SR 1528).

7.1 Turn left onto Talley Road (SR 1527).

10.2 Talley Road name changes to Pleasant Grove Road.

11.6 Pleasant Grove Road curves to right; name changes again to River Road.

18.3 Turn right onto Big Willow Road (SR 1191).

23.5 Turn right onto Crab Creek Road (SR 1528).

31.9 Pass intersection with Talley Road.

32.6 Turn left onto Old Hendersonville Road (SR 1504).

35.7 Continue straight on Old Hendersonville Road (SR 1533), which runs into SR 1533.

36.6 Cross bridge over French Broad River.

38.4 Turn left onto U.S. 64/276.

39.0 Arrive at parking lot at intersection of Broad and French Broad Streets.

graduate curricula. The original school on this site, Rutherford Academy, was founded by Robert Abernathy around 1858. The school became Rutherford College in 1870 after having closed twice during the Civil War. It was taken over by the Methodist Episcopal Church in 1900 and then merged with Weaver College to form Brevard College in 1942.

French Broad River Loop:
Transylvania County

Number of miles:	16.75
Approximate pedaling time:	1½ hours
Terrain:	Rolling
Traffic:	Heavy along U.S. 64/276 but light on the back roads
Things to see:	Brevard, Brevard College, mountains, French Broad River, farms, wildflowers
Food:	Restaurants and grocery stores in Brevard

Transylvania County in southwestern North Carolina prides itself on being one of the state's most beautiful counties, with its rugged mountain peaks and gorgeous river valleys. More than half the county is included in either the Pisgah National Forest (83,000 acres) or the Nantahala National Forest (5,000 acres).

The magnificent variations in altitude—from 1,025 feet at the lowest point to 6,045 feet on Tanassee Bald—create more than 250 waterfalls in the county, more than any other county in the United States. Waterfall guidebooks are available from both the National Forest Service and bookstores in the area.

Amazingly enough in light of the surrounding terrain, this route is not difficult, because it wanders through the French Broad River valley, hugging the river along much of the route. It ranges from tree-shaded lanes through country roads, passing lovely pastures with a profusion of wildflowers blooming along the roadside in the warm months. Throughout the ride you have wonderful views of the mountains that surround this peaceful valley.

As you prepare to begin, be sure to note the impressive stone

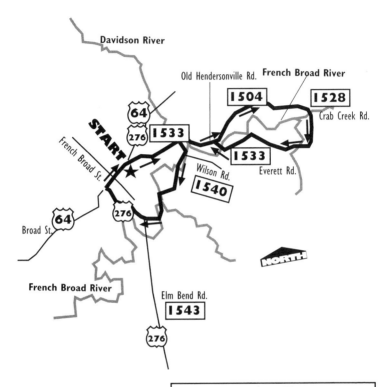

Davidson River

Old Hendersonville Rd. **French Broad River**

1504

1528

Crab Creek Rd.

64

276

1533

1533

Everett Rd.

START

French Broad St.

Wilson Rd.

1540

64

276

Broad St.

NORTH

French Broad River

Elm Bend Rd.

1543

276

Getting There

From U.S. 64 coming into Brevard, head west toward Brevard College downtown on Broad Street (U.S. 64/276). Shopping center parking lot is at intersection of Broad and French Broad Streets across from college.

DIRECTIONS at a glance

0.0 From traffic signal by parking lot at intersection of Broad Street (U.S. 64/276) and French Broad Street in downtown Brevard, across from Brevard College, turn right onto Broad Street (U.S. 64/276).

0.6 Bear right on Old Hendersonville Road (SR 1533). (U.S. 64/276 goes off to the left.)

2.4 Cross bridge over the French Broad River

3.3 Bear left onto SR 1504 (Old Hendersonville Road).

6.4 Turn right onto Crab Creek Road (SR 1528).

7.7 Turn right onto Everett Road (SR 1533).

10.9 Turn left onto Old Hendersonville Road (SR 1533).

12.0 Turn left onto Wilson Road (SR 1540), about 0.2 miles after crossing the bridge.

14.6 Turn right onto Elm Bend Road (SR 1543).

15.7 Turn right onto U.S. 276.

15.9 Turn right, staying on U.S. 276.

16.5 At intersection, turn right onto Broad Street (U.S. 64/276).

16.75 Turn right into parking lot.

wall surrounding the Brevard College campus. The wall and arch are listed on the National Register of Historic Places.

Along SR 1528 and SR 1533, you'll see stone houses that use the indigenous river rocks for their solid construction and give them a type of camouflage with the locale. Along SR 1533 (Everett Road), horses graze lazily on the lush green grasses growing in the rich soil of the riverbank. At 6.5 miles the road kisses the river bank and you have great views of the gently gurgling river, which is not very deep but spreads wide in places.

As you swing south of Brevard along Wilson Road (SR 1540), you'll pass the Glen Cannon Golf Course. Bright orange daylilies line the road's edge in summer and buffer the road from the verdant pastures. The gentle ups and downs of the route appear minor when compared to the steep hillsides all around the valley. Along Elm Bend Road you'll see neatly tended vegetable gardens in the small communities that periodically people the route.

U.S. 64/276 takes you right through the main part of downtown Brevard, with its tree-shaded streets and inviting front porches. The charming old downtown area is perfect for strolling or lounging in one of the many cafes.

In summer Brevard teems with visitors as musicians from across the country gather for the internationally renowned Brevard Music Festival, which runs from late June through mid-August. Concurrent with the festival is a summer camp to provide quality music education for talented young people. A steady schedule of more than fifty concerts and operas attracts tens of thousands of visitors to the festival's covered amphitheater, which seats about 1,500. This influx means that area restaurants stay busy and reservations are advised during these weeks of the festival.

Founded in 1936 by Dr. James Christian Pfohl, the Music Center began as a summer camp for boys. Dr. Pfohl, a music professor at Davidson College, decided that the college's music facilities should be used during the summer months. Summer sessions were held on the Davidson College campus until World War II began and all the campus was needed for military barracks. The operation moved then to Queens College, a women's college in Charlotte, and became coeducational. The search for the perfect setting for the program of outdoor recreation and instruction for music and art led to the establishment of the Music Center in Brevard. The Music Festival was conceived in 1946 and is still going strong.

Ride to Whitewater Falls:
Transylvania County

Number of miles:	17.2
Approximate pedaling time:	2 hours
Terrain:	Hilly
Traffic:	Sometimes heavy
Things to see:	Horsepasture River, Whitewater Falls, forests, wildlife, mountains
Food:	Limited number of stores in Sapphire, which is between Cashiers and Lake Toxaway, where there are more sources

Whitewater Falls, the highest cascade east of the Mississippi River, forms the dividing line between Jackson and Transylvania counties, and both claim it. The water tumbles steeply over large boulders in tiers to the floor 411 feet below. The Cherokee name for the falls was Charashilactay, which meant "white water." The spectacular view of the falls from below greets visitors to the scenic area who walk about .25 mile from the parking area. More adventurous souls can hike a steep trail to the top of the falls. This vantage point gets you closer to the falls, but the view is not nearly as breathtaking as that from the bottom. These sights make the rather strenuous trip well worth the effort.

Keep that in mind as you start the ride, because the first climb comes at 1.6 miles and continues for 0.7 mile. At 2.2 miles you'll cross the Horsepasture River, which itself hosts numerous waterfalls. Another climb—0.6 mile in length—awaits you at 3.5 miles. You might want to take a breather at the Mountain Crafts Gallery at 5.3 miles.

At 7.2 miles you enter the Nantahala National Forest and 0.6 mile later cross the Whitewater River, which feeds the falls. At 8.6 miles you'll see the sign for the Nantahala National Forest Whitewater Falls Scenic Area on your left. A short road brings you to the ranger hut and parking area. There are rest rooms and water sources here. When the ranger is on duty during the busy summer months, you pay a modest user's fee ($2.00 to $3.00) to enter the park.

The falls are actually situated on the boundary between what are now Jackson and Transylvania counties, and both claim it as a local attraction. This situation amounts to friendly sharing compared to the bitter battle between North Carolina and Georgia over the exact locations of the states' common boundary. The battle started early in the nineteenth century when with the increasing population in the area, it became more important to establish property lines and state boundaries. In the Transylvania-Jackson region, the matter was complicated because many people held land grants from both North Carolina and Georgia.

The state of Georgia, believing its northern boundary to run along the thirty-fifth degree north latitude, created Walton County there while North Carolina claimed the same area. Both states were performing governmental actions in the same area at the same time. According to historian Martin Skaggs, the opposition became active and violent; administrative officials were beaten and abused, and it was impossible to collect taxes. These chaotic conditions attracted outlaws and violent refugees who further added to the confusion. There was even an armed confrontation between governmental forces on each side around 1810. The Carolinas won those battles and, as a result, Georgia's northern boundary was moved so far west that it does not even touch Transylvania County today. The issue was even resurrected in 1971 when Georgia named a legislative commission to study the issue. North Carolina legislators from the area jumped to the defense. Fortunately, both states' proposals died in committee. Otherwise, Whitewater Falls might be in Georgia.

64

START

281

NORTH

Horse Pasture River

Whitewater River

SOUTH CAROLINA

Whitewater Falls
Scenic Park

Getting There

From Brevard, take U.S. 64 east to Sapphire; from Cashiers, take U.S. 64 west. Park in Sapphire at businesses along U.S. 64.

DIREC-TIONS at a glance

0.0 From parking at businesses along U.S. 64 in Sapphire, turn right and head south on NC–281.

2.2 Cross Horsepasture River.

5.3 Pass Mountain Crafts Gallery.

7.2 Enter Nantahala National Forest.

7.8 Cross Whitewater River.

8.6 Turn left into Scenic Area for Whitewater Falls. Turn around and retrace route.

17.2 Return to Sapphire.

Hunting Country Tour:
Polk County

Number of miles:	22.4 (35.6 with optional side trip)
Approximate pedaling time:	3 hours (5 hours with optional side trip)
Terrain:	Rolling to very hilly; optional side trip is a 6-mile climb
Traffic:	Light to moderate along U.S. 176 and NC–108
Things to see:	Large horse farms, hardwood forests, FENCE (Foothills Equestrian Nature Center), Pacolet River, mountain homes, Pearson's Falls Natural Heritage Site, Historic Polk County Courthouse, Historic Saluda
Food:	Restaurants and stores in towns of Columbus, Tryon, and Saluda

Polk County, situated in the Carolina Foothills, serves as a gateway to Asheville and the mountains to the west. Before you begin riding, take a moment to study the historic Polk County Courthouse. Built by slaves in 1857, it holds a place in the National Register of Historic Places and still has the original slave block out front.

Much of this route traverses horse country, as you can tell by the names. The hardwood forests along Peniel Street (SR 1521) break to present the first large horse farms as you turn onto Red Fox Road (SR 1519). Immaculate white horse fences line this section of the route, punctuated with yellow caution signs warning about horses and carriages in the area. Along Hunting Country Road (SR 1501) after 4.8 miles, you're rewarded with a great vista to your left before you cross the creek.

Amazing blankets of kudzu encroach on the road and you

47

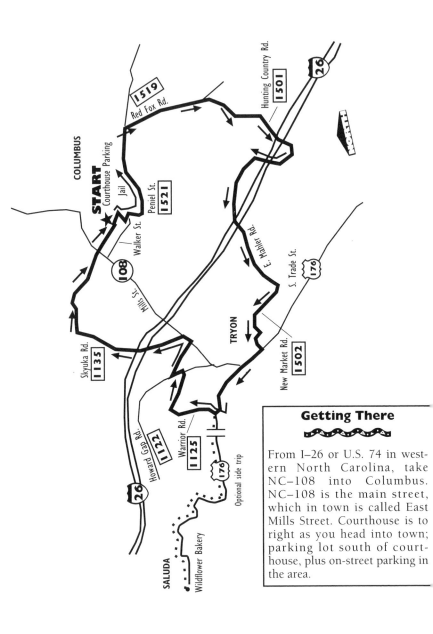

COLUMBUS

START
Courthouse Parking

Jail

Walker St.

Peniel St. **1521**

Red Fox Rd. **1519**

Hunting Country Rd. **1501**

26

E. Mahler Rd.

S. Trade St. **176**

108

Mills St.

TRYON

New Market Rd. **1502**

Skyuka Rd. **1135**

Howard Gap Rd. **1122**

Warrior Rd. **1125**

176

Optional side trip

26

SALUDA

Wildflower Bakery

Getting There

From I–26 or U.S. 74 in western North Carolina, take NC–108 into Columbus. NC–108 is the main street, which in town is called East Mills Street. Courthouse is to right as you head into town; parking lot south of courthouse, plus on-street parking in the area.

DIREC-TIONS at a glance

0.0 From front of courthouse on East Mills Street in Columbus (parking available on street and in lot), exit to right to stop sign in front of jail. Turn right at stop sign, then left at next stop sign onto Walker Street.

0.1 Turn right onto Peniel Street (SR 1521).

1.4 Bear left, staying on Peniel Street.

2.8 Turn right onto Red Fox Road (SR 1519).

4.8 Turn right onto Hunting Country Road (SR 1501).

5.6 Cross creek and bear left around a 90-degree curve.

6.0 Cross over I–26.

6.7 Turn right onto E. Mahler Road (SR 1501).

7.2 Follow sharp right curve.

8.0 Cross under I–26.

8.8 Cross I–26 for third time.

11.0 Turn right onto New Market Road (SR 1502), which passes through Tryon.

12.9 Turn right onto South Trade Street (U.S. 176).

13.4 Veer left onto U.S. 176 West.

14.5 Turn right onto Warrior Road (SR 1125). (Optional side trip to Saluda begins and ends at this point.)

17.0 Turn left onto Howard Gap Road (SR 1122).

17.2 Turn right onto Old Howard Gap Road (SR 1122)

18.0 Turn left onto NC–108.

18.3 Turn left onto Skyuka Road (SR 1135).

22.3 Turn left onto East Mills Street.

22.4 Turn right into courthouse parking lot.

13.2 miles

14.5 For optional side trip to Saluda, do not turn onto Warrior Road. Instead, continue west on U.S. 176.

18.2 Pearson's Falls overlook.

21.1 Enter main part of Saluda. Turn around at Wildflour Bakery and retrace route.

27.7 Turn left onto Warrior Road and resume original tour.

can almost imagine it spreading before your very eyes. Farms in the area sport names like Red Fox and Breezy Hill. A half-mile after you turn onto SR 1501, the road curves sharply and leads to FENCE, the Foothills Equestrian Nature Center. This 300-acre nature preserve incorporates hiking and riding trails, picnic areas, and a pond with boardwalk. Open to the public year-round, the facility hosts equestrian events, concerts, and private gatherings in its lodge. Its large and natural setting makes it perfect for bird-watching.

At 8.8 miles, after you once again cross I–26, Chinquapin Farm spreads out against a glorious mountain backdrop. New Market Road's curvy and somewhat rough surface looks down on cornfields in the valley before climbing through a residential area into Tryon. The town's Thermal Belt—an unusual microclimate that is usually free of dew and frost—ensures a pleasant atmosphere, whatever the season, although the surrounding hills change colors to mark time's passing.

A North Carolina Scenic Byway, U.S. 176 keeps pace with the Pacolet River as it marches past lovely mountain retreats, dense forests barely eclipsing the mountains that lie behind. At the intersection of U.S. 176 and Warrior Road at 14.5 miles, you face the decision of turning and continuing the basic ride or testing your mettle with the optional climb into Saluda. Don't let the flat stretch at the beginning fool you. But if your legs and lungs can handle it, Saluda is well worth the effort.

Called a "town the railroad built," Saluda nestles at the crest of the Saluda Grade, the steepest mainline railroad grade in the United States. Fortunately an extra climbing lane provides extra space for cyclists going into Saluda, and signs along the route encourage motorists to share the road with bicycles. About halfway up the grade, if you need to rest for a moment, a perfect stopping point overlooks Pearson's Falls on the Pacolet River.

Other visual respites along the way come from tiny waterfalls tumbling over massive rocks to the road's edge and streams that crisscross the highway. Log houses and artisans shops such as Fig Falls Pottery and Valhalla Hand Weavers pique your curiosity. Your strenuous efforts are rewarded when you arrive at the Wildflour Bakery in Saluda, the favorite stopping point for cyclists from a broad area around Polk County. Operated as a co-operative run by a few dozen women, the shop tempts you with freshly baked sticky buns and other delicious offerings. Outside tables allow you to enjoy both the goodies and the view when the weather's nice.

Saluda's downtown area remains much as it looked in the past and is honored with a listing on the National Register of Historic Places. Two walking tours are mapped out or you can just stroll around before you head down the mountain.

Kings Mountain Tour:
Gaston County

Number of miles:	26.7
Approximate pedaling time:	2½ hours
Terrain:	Rolling, with some good hills
Traffic:	Light
Things to see:	Crowders Mountain, Kings Mountain, the Kings Mountain National Military Park
Food:	Convenience stores along SC–161

The starting point for this tour, Crowders Mountain State Park, offers 2,586 acres of parkland with facilities for camping, picnicking, hiking, and fishing. Nature programs are also offered.

This tour connects three parks and travels one scenic byway through southernmost North Carolina, dipping slightly into South Carolina. Sparrow Springs Road, the Scenic Byway, climbs slightly through the woods of the park and then passes through a residential area. Lewis Road is curvy, with all styles of homes tucked into the woods on either side.

The part of Unity Church Road we're traveling is paved, although you'll see where the pavement ends. Battleground Road curves through farmland and woods as it leads to Kings Mountain. You'll know when you've crossed the state line into South Carolina because the road surface becomes more uneven and narrower. When you cross SC–161, Battleground Road's name changes to Park Road.

Kings Mountain State Park, consisting of 6,471 acres of land, offers a broad range of outdoor activities, including boating, fishing, swimming, and hiking. You can get more information at

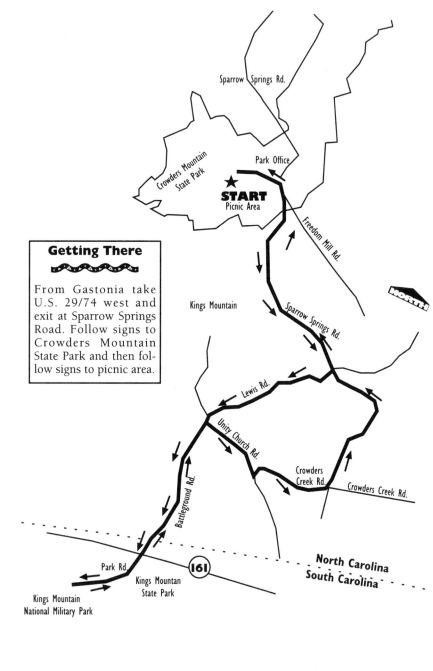

Sparrow Springs Rd.

Crowders Mountain State Park

Park Office

★ **START**
Picnic Area

Freedom Mill Rd.

NORTH

Getting There

From Gastonia take U.S. 29/74 west and exit at Sparrow Springs Road. Follow signs to Crowders Mountain State Park and then follow signs to picnic area.

Kings Mountain

Sparrow Springs Rd.

Lewis Rd.

Unity Church Rd.

Battleground Rd.

Crowders Creek Rd.

Crowders Creek Rd.

161

Park Rd.

Kings Mountain State Park

North Carolina
South Carolina

Kings Mountain National Military Park

0.0 From picnic parking area at end of road in Crowders Mountain State Park, turn right.

0.3 Park office on left.

0.5 Turn right onto Sparrow Springs Road. Continue on Sparrow Springs Road at the intersection with Freedom Mill Road, bearing right.

4.3 Turn right onto Lewis Road.

4.9 Turn left onto Unity Church Road.

5.0 Turn right onto Battleground Road.

6.1 Cross state line into South Carolina.

7.9 Cross SC–161, where Battleground Road name changes to Park Road, and continue on Park Road into Kings Mountain State Park.

11.7 Turn right into Visitors Center for Kings Mountain National Military Park. When you exit after your visit, turn left onto Park Road. Continue back on Park Road through Kings Mountain State Park.

15.5 Cross SC–161. Park Road name changes to Battleground Road.

16.3 Stay on Battleground Road as you cross state line back into North Carolina.

17.4 Turn right onto Unity Church Road.

18.2 Turn left onto Crowders Creek Road.

19.1 Turn left onto Sparrow Springs Road.

22.2 View of Crowders Mountain on left.

26.2 Turn left into Crowders Mountain State Park.

26.7 Turn left into parking area.

the Visitors Center. Also in the park is a restored 1840s homestead called the Living History Farm.

The destination of this ride is Kings Mountain National Military Park, one of the largest military parks in the United States.

Kings Mountain is a rocky, wooded, outlying spur of the Blue Ridge Mountains, rising some 60 feet above the surrounding plain. A plateau at its summit about 600 yards long provided an excellent campsite and defensive position for Major Patrick Ferguson, leader of the British and Loyalist forces during the American Revolution.

Under the command of General Cornwallis, who had easily overrun South Carolina after his resounding win in Charleston, Ferguson was ordered to invade the upcountry of South Carolina. He succeeded in recruiting several thousand Carolinians of loyal British persuasion. Ferguson's opponents were the Over-Mountain Men who hailed from the mountainous areas of Virginia, North Carolina, and South Carolina, remote areas that had been little affected by the five-year-old war. Once threatened, however, they proved their mettle by hiking through deep snow and pouring rain to finally catch up with Ferguson at Kings Mountain.

Although outnumbered by the better-trained Loyalists, the Over-Mountain Men remained undaunted, joining forces and forming a horseshoe around the base of the mountain. The Loyalists were taken completely by surprise. The mountain men steadily advanced against repeated bayonet charges and eventually captured the summit. Ferguson, conspicuous in his checkered hunting shirt, was fatally shot from his horse. The Loyalists surrendered, flagging the spirits of their comrades and leading to Cornwallis's defeat at Guilford Courthouse the next year.

Ferguson was buried on the summit. A Scotsman, Ferguson's remains are marked with a Scottish cairn, a pile of rocks. Local legend has it that American visitors to the site should carry a rock to the summit to place on this cairn, to ensure that Ferguson has no chance to do further harm to the Carolinas.

The Kings Mountain Military Park Visitors Center has an audiovisual presentation on the battle, and a self-guided walking tour shows different aspects of the battle as well as various monuments to those who died here.

At the end of this bike tour, Crowders Mountain provides the perfect spot to cool off and recover from the ride.

Queen City Tour:
Charlotte

Number of miles:	18.5 (13.8 for shorter loop)
Approximate pedaling time:	2 hours
Terrain:	Rolling
Traffic:	Can be heavy downtown and on busier streets; most of this tour covers side streets
Things to see:	Ericsson Stadium, Mint Museum, NationsBank building with murals, Queens College, Nature Museum, older Charlotte neighborhoods, City Hall, BB&T Bank Building, First Citizens Bank, Charlotte skyline, fountains, outdoor sculptures
Food:	Lots of options at SouthPark Mall and in downtown area

Charlotte, the largest city in the Carolinas, was named in honor of Queen Charlotte of Mecklenburg-Strelitz, wife of King George III of England. She is also the source of its nickname: the Queen City. As these names indicate, Charlotte initially had very strong ties to England and the British Crown. But those ties were broken in 1775 with the signing of the Mecklenburg Resolves, which invalidated the authority of the English king and Parliament.

Lord Cornwallis, who occupied the town for several days in 1780, called it a "hornet's nest of rebellion" because of the intense activity by the Patriots. The story and the name have held through the years. Most recently the professional basketball team in Charlotte has taken the name Hornets.

Charlotte is also known as the City of Trees. Although Hurricane Hugo did terrible damage to the urban forest in the fall of 1989, you can still see why the city got that nickname as you enjoy this tour through many of Charlotte's loveliest tree-shaded neighborhoods. The SouthPark area where the ride starts has become the chic shopping district, so you'll see many interesting boutiques and restaurants mixed with the usual chain stores.

After you turn on Barclay Downs, you'll pass lovely residential areas, many with stately older homes. At 3.1 miles, you turn onto Queens Road East. With its partner—Queens Road West, of course—this street forms a large oval through the lovely Myers Park neighborhood. Queens Road is a divided four-lane with a tree-lined median and very large homes gracing its sides.

At 5.3 miles Providence Road curves left and becomes Third Street as you head into Uptown Charlotte—which most people would recognize as downtown. Whether you call it up or down, it's the center of town. A shorter tour turns off around this point to avoid the busiest part of Uptown. If you stay on the original route, you'll have a great view at 5.7 miles of the Charlotte skyline, which is dominated by the NationsBank building. At 6.0 miles you can admire the large Corinthian columns and classical architecture of the Mecklenburg County Courthouse.

As you turn right on Stonewall Street, the *Charlotte Observer* newspaper building is to your left. Straight ahead looms Ericsson Stadium, home of the Charlotte Panthers football team. South Mint Street becomes a one-way from the opposite direction within the next couple of blocks, so you'll take a diagonal to Poplar Street to get to Trade Street, the principal east-west street in Uptown. Riding along Trade Street will help you understand why Charlotte is becoming one of the nation's largest financial centers as you encounter the towers of NationsBank and First Union Bank, major banks headquartered in Charlotte.

The NationsBank Tower and Corporate Center are located at the intersection of Trade and Tryon Streets, which is called the Square. It's the historic crossroads of the city and the site of its founding more than 250 years ago. This intersection, one of the

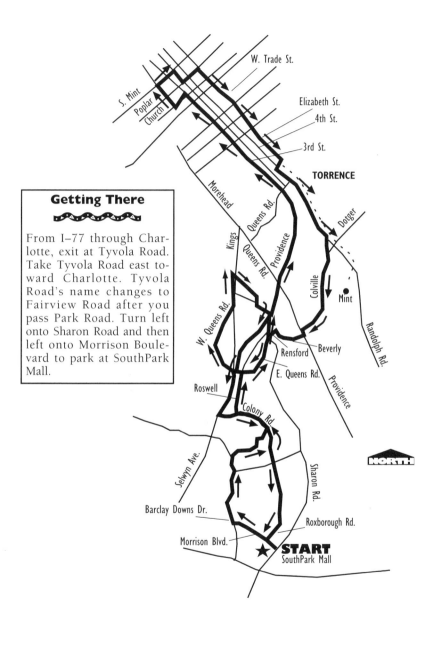

W. Trade St.

S. Mint

Poplar

Church

Elizabeth St.

4th St.

3rd St.

TORRENCE

Morehead

Queens Rd.

Dotger

Kings

Queens Rd.

Providence

Colville

Mint

Getting There

From I–77 through Charlotte, exit at Tyvola Road. Take Tyvola Road east toward Charlotte. Tyvola Road's name changes to Fairview Road after you pass Park Road. Turn left onto Sharon Road and then left onto Morrison Boulevard to park at SouthPark Mall.

W. Queens Rd.

Randolph Rd.

Rensford

Beverly

E. Queens Rd.

Providence

Roswell

Colony Rd.

Selwyn Ave.

Sharon Rd.

Barclay Downs Dr.

Roxborough Rd.

Morrison Blvd.

★ **START**
SouthPark Mall

NORTH

DIRECTIONS at a glance

0.0 From SouthPark Mall on Morrison Boulevard at the intersection with Roxborough Road, turn left onto Morrison Boulevard.

0.3 Turn right onto Barclay Downs.

1.0 Turn left onto Runnymede.

1.2 Turn right into Myers Park High School property, bear right, and then veer left to main entrance on Colony Road.

1.8 Turn left at Y-intersection onto Colony Road.

2.7 Turn right onto Roswell Avenue.

3.1 Turn right onto Queens Road West.

3.8 Bear right on Queens Road at five-point intersection.

4.3 Go straight on Providence Road. (Queens Road goes off to left.)

5.3 Providence Road curves left and becomes Third Street.

7.0 Turn left onto Church Street.

7.3 Turn right onto Stonewall Street.

7.4 Turn right onto South Mint Street. Bear right onto South Poplar. (South Mint becomes one way at this point.)

7.8 Turn right onto West Trade Street.

8.7 West Trade Street name changes to Elizabeth Street.

9.0 Turn right onto Torrence Street.

9.1 Turn left onto East Fourth Street, the name of which changes to Randolph Road.

10.2 Turn right onto Museum Drive into the Mint Museum. Circle around and return to entrance.

10.6 At Mint Museum entrance, turn left onto Randolph Road.

10.9 Turn left onto Dotger Avenue.

11.0 Turn left onto Colville Road.

12.0 Turn left onto Providence Road.

12.1 Turn right onto Beverly Drive.

12.4 Turn left onto Rensford Avenue.

12.5 Turn right onto Sharon Road, then make an immediate left onto Queens Road East.

13.6 Continue straight; Queens Road East becomes Kings Road.

14.4 Turn right onto Norton Road and cross Queens Road West.

14.8 Turn right onto Hertford Road, then left onto Sherwood Avenue.

15.0 Turn right onto Queens Road, then bear right on Selwyn Avenue.

16.4 Turn left onto Colony Road.

16.9 Tricky intersection!! At the entrance to Myers Park High School, the road is blocked the way you want to go, so turn right into the school, go to second median, and make a U-turn so you can go right on Colony Road.

17.1 Turn right onto Colony Road.

18.2 Turn right onto Roxborough Road.

18.5 Intersection with Morrison Boulevard; return to South-Park Mall.

13.8 miles

5.3 Just before where Providence Road curves to left and becomes Third Street, turn right on Colonial Avenue.

6.7 Turn right on Randolph Road and pick up original tour at 10.2 miles, approaching Mint Museum.

---

loveliest anywhere, stands out because of its many varied fountains and large outdoor sculptures. Although the 60-story NationsBank Tower has no observation deck, you should take a few minutes to visit the magnificent lobby to view the three huge frescoes by Ben Long that were commissioned especially for this building. Each measures 23 by 18 feet.

The Museum of the New South is located 1 block east of this intersection. The Mint Museum, the next major stop, is located east on Fourth Street/Randolph Road. The museum is housed in a building constructed from materials used in the original Charlotte Mint, formerly located on Mint Street. Opened in 1837 and producing more than $5 million in coins—many using gold from area mines—until the Civil War, the original building was purchased, measured, and demolished. After it was reconstructed it became the Mint Museum.

Iron Forge Tour:
Lincoln County

Number of miles:	42.2
Approximate pedaling time:	4 hours
Terrain:	Rolling
Traffic:	Light on the secondary roads to moderate or heavy along NC–73
Things to see:	Lake Norman, historic homes, rural communities and farms, Iron Station
Food:	Along NC–73, primarily on the east side of Lake Norman but also around 8.4 miles, and in Iron Station

This route, which coincides with part of the North Carolina Mountains to Sea Bicycle Route 6 along NC–73, provides an interesting juxtaposition of rural and resort or residential development as you ride west from Lake Norman. This body of water, 8 miles wide and 30 miles long, is the largest inland and artificially created lake in North Carolina, offering 520 miles of shoreline. Its proximity to Charlotte has made it an attractive location for Charlotte commuters and those seeking a weekend retreat. Its development started on the east side, close to Interstate 77, but has since spread to all other parts of the lake as well.

This tour gives you an excellent vantage point of the lake, away from the higher-traffic areas. Duke Power Company's Energy Explorium is the starting point. After you turn on Club Drive (SR 1395), you have a great view of Cowans Ford Dam, which created the lake, and Duke Power's McGuire Nuclear Power Plant. Cowans Ford Country Club is to your left. After 3.7 miles the lake is bordered by large homes. A quick side trip

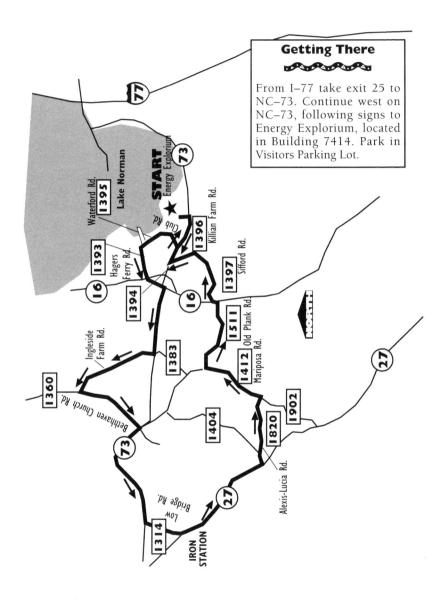

Getting There

From I-77 take exit 25 to NC-73. Continue west on NC-73, following signs to Energy Explorium, located in Building 7414. Park in Visitors Parking Lot.

0.0 From the Visitors Parking Lot at Duke Power's Energy Explorium off NC–73, follow the main road back to NC–73.

0.7 Turn right onto NC–73.

2.7 Turn right onto Club Drive (SR 1395).

5.4 Turn right onto Waterford Road. Circle around and return to Club Drive.

6.1 Turn right onto Club Drive (SR 1395) and then bear left onto Hagers Ferry Road (SR 1393).

7.7 After you cross SR 1394, turn left onto NC–16.

8.4 Turn right onto NC–73.

10.9 Turn right onto Ingleside Farm Road (SR 1383).

14.2 Turn left onto Bethhaven Church Road (SR 1360).

17.0 Turn right onto NC–73 (sign for Bike Route 6).

21.1 Turn left onto Low Bridge Road (SR 1314).

22.6 Turn left onto NC–27 into Iron Station.

26.8 Turn left onto Alexis-Lucia Road (SR 1820).

27.3 Bear right on Alexis-Lucia Road. (SR 1404 goes off to left.)

29.9 Turn left onto Mariposa Road (SR 1412).

32.3 Turn right onto Old Plank Road (SR 1511). *Note:* No name sign at turn.

35.1 Turn left onto NC–16.

35.3 Turn right onto Sifford Road (SR 1397).

37.5 Turn left at stop sign onto Killian Farm Road (SR 1396). *Note:* No name sign at turn.

38.7 Turn right onto NC–73.

41.5 Turn left into Duke Power's Energy Explorium grounds.

42.2 Return to parking lot.

down Waterford Road gives you a good view of one of the many coves with sailboats tied up at family docks.

After you rejoin NC–73 it provides some nice ups and downs, especially a nice downhill around 9.0 miles. Take care because the shoulderless road has heavier traffic than is desirable for cycling. Ingleside Farm Road (SR 1383) at 10.9 miles takes you past old farmhouses and pastures. The Ingleside properties once belonged to a family prominent in the iron industry in Lincoln County. The Ingleside home, located west of SR 1383 off the road a ways, is listed in the National Register of Historic Places.

At 14.2 miles along Bethhaven Church Road are two unusual sites: a round barn and a wooden shantytown built around a quadrangle. Look for a historic home on NC–73 at about 18.5 miles.

You arrive in Iron Station at 22.6 miles, the town so named because of the successful iron industry that flourished in the county in the early nineteenth century. In 1823 ten forges and four furnaces were producing bar iron and castings in the form of skillets, pots, pans, and irons, and ovens for local trade. The isolation of the area at that time made the industry necessary, but it declined as better and cheaper products became more readily available from the north.

Old Plank Road (SR 1511) at 32.3 miles recalls the plank roads that eventually connected this area with settlements and towns to the east. Duke Power's Lincoln Turbine Station is to the left.

At 38.7 miles you rejoin NC–73 to return to the Energy Explorium. You again see Cowans Ford Dam from a different vantage point to your left just before you cross the Catawba River. Lake Norman is visible through the trees, as is the McGuire Nuclear Power Plant.

If you're interested in visiting the Energy Explorium, it's open free of charge Monday through Saturday from 9:00 A.M. to 5:00 P.M. and on Sunday from noon to 5:00 P.M.

Bruce's Tour of Historic Salisbury

Number of miles:	10.1
Approximate pedaling time:	1½ hours
Terrain:	Mainly rolling, with flat stretches
Traffic:	Moderate, even along Main and Innes Streets
Things to see:	Many historic houses in the Salisbury Historic District, North Carolina Transportation Museum, Presbyterian Bell Tower
Food:	Many restaurants and stores in Salisbury and Spencer

Named after the cathedral town in England, Salisbury was chartered in 1755 as the county seat of Rowan County. Its location at the convergence of the Trading Path from eastern Virginia and the Great Pennsylvania Wagon Road spurred economic development in the area that was further increased by the coming of the railroad in the mid-1800s. Salisbury's 30-block historic district encompasses all styles of elegant homes from times past. Fortunately the town, its courthouse, and private residences were spared the wrath of Union General George Stoneman, supposedly because both he and the mayor of Salisbury were Masons.

The first part of this tour winds past historic residences (not open to the public). The Wilson-Crawford House at 207 South Ellis Street was built in 1853 in the Federal style by a local silversmith. The Heilig House (507 South Fulton Street, at the corner shared with West Monroe Street) was built in 1865 by a partner in the Gold Hill gold mine. The original detached

kitchen remains on the site, believed to be the oak grove where General Stoneman's troops camped.

The Josephus Hall House at 226 South Jackson Street was once home to Chief Surgeon Hall of the Salisbury Confederate Prison during the Civil War. Built in 1820 in the Federal style, additions in 1859—including the cast-iron verandas—and in 1900 gave the house Greek Revival and Victorian features. Housed in the building is an important collection of Victorian furnishings and accessories as well as the house's original fixtures.

The Craige House at 329 West Bank Street, constructed in 1877 in the Italianate style, remains in the Craige family to this day. It was built by Kerr Craige, assistant postmaster general, whose father introduced the Ordinance of Secession that took North Carolina out of the Union. The houses at 201 South Fulton Street and 301 West Fisher Street represent two outstanding examples of the Spanish mission style in residential architecture.

In the block before you reach West Innes Street, you'll see the Salisbury Female Academy building at 115 South Jackson Street. Built in 1839, it's one of the oldest academy buildings in North Carolina. The 1892 Presbyterian Bell Tower near the intersection of Jackson and Innes Streets is all that remains of the Richardsonian Romanesque First Presbyterian Church. It now symbolizes preservation efforts in Salisbury and Rowan County.

When you turn left onto Main Street from Innes Street, the Kluttz Drug Store Building will be on your right. This three-story structure was the tallest commercial building in North Carolina when it was built in 1858.

Salisbury's spacious Main Street takes you past all sorts of shops, restaurants, and businesses before it becomes Salisbury Street in Spencer. This town, once the site of Southern Railway's largest steam locomotive repair shops, is now home to the North Carolina Transportation Museum as well as numerous other businesses and shops.

The museum pays tribute to the golden years of the railroad with displays of elegant private rail cars, a massive locomotive on a turntable, its 1924 Bob Julian Roundhouse, and the volun-

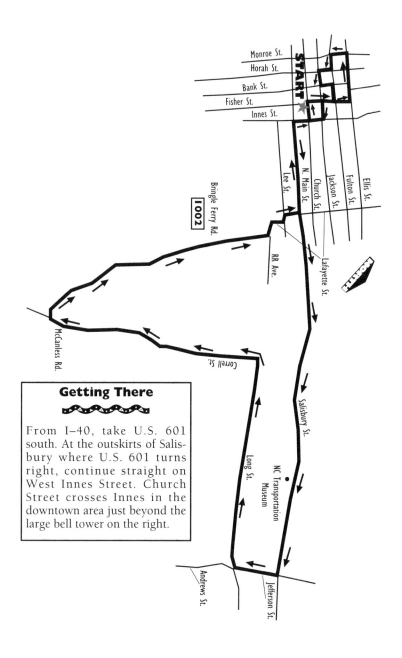

Monroe St.

Horah St.

START

Bank St.

Fisher St.

Innes St.

Lee St.

N. Main St.

Church St.

Jackson St.

Fulton St.

Ellis St.

Bringle Ferry Rd.

1002

RR Ave.

Lafayette St.

McCanless Rd.

Correll St.

Salisbury St.

Getting There

From I–40, take U.S. 601 south. At the outskirts of Salisbury where U.S. 601 turns right, continue straight on West Innes Street. Church Street crosses Innes in the downtown area just beyond the large bell tower on the right.

Long St.

NC Transportation Museum

Andrews St.

Jefferson St.

DIREC-TIONS at a glance

0.0 From intersection of South Church Street and West Fisher Street in downtown Salisbury, turn right onto West Fisher Street.

0.2 Turn left onto South Ellis Street.

0.4 Turn left onto West Monroe Street.

0.5 Turn left onto South Fulton Street.

0.6 Turn right onto West Horah Street.

0.7 Turn left onto South Jackson Street (a one-way street).

0.8 Turn left onto West Bank Street.

0.9 Turn right onto South Fulton Street.

1.0 Turn right onto West Fisher Street.

1.1 Turn left onto South Jackson Street.

1.2 Turn right onto West Innes Street.

1.3 Turn left onto North Main Street. The name changes to Salisbury Street when you enter Spencer.

4.1 Turn right into North Carolina Transportation Museum. Exit museum, going right onto Salisbury Street.

4.4 Turn right onto Andrews Street.

4.6 Turn right onto North Long Street.

5.7 Turn left onto Correll Street. The name changes to McCanless Road.

6.4 Cross one-lane bridge.

7.2 Turn right onto Bringle Ferry Road (SR 1002).

9.3 Turn left onto Railroad Avenue, then immediately right onto East Lafayette Street.

9.4 Turn left onto Lee Street, then immediately right onto East Lafayette Street.

9.5 Turn left onto North Main Street.

10.0 Turn right onto West Innes Street.

10.1 Turn left onto South Church Street and return to West Fisher Street intersection.

teer railroad buffs who work to preserve America's steam loco-motives. But you'll also find much more there. You can examine the Original North Carolina Highway Patrol car—a convertible, no less—along with other antique automobile displays. Other forms of transportation, including bicycles and dugout canoes, are also on display. Train rides from the museum start at three or four designated times each day. A fee is charged for the rides, but admission to the museum is free.

The return route loops through the countryside on the out-skirts of Salisbury before following Lafayette Street back to Main Street.

Hanging Rock Loop:
Stokes County

Number of miles:	20.7
Approximate pedaling time:	2½ hours
Terrain:	Very hilly to rolling
Traffic:	Minimal, except on NC–8/89 and NC–66
Things to see:	Hanging Rock, Hanging Rock State Park, Sauratown Mountain, Flat Shoals Mountain, great sweeping vistas
Food:	In Danbury and at Singletree Inn and Restaurant off Moores Springs Road

You won't have to worry about getting lost in Danbury, the county seat of Stokes County and home to one hundred residents. NC–8/89 is the one main street through town, and the hilly terrain minimizes the number of roads that sprout off the main route.

Moratock Park takes its name from Moratock Furnace, a smelting furnace built by Nathaniel Moody in 1843 that supplied iron to the Confederacy from 1862 to 1865. Danbury itself was an important landmark during the war because Union General George Stoneman set up his headquarters here on April 9, 1865, the day General Robert E. Lee surrendered at Appomattox. Stoneman's name was popularized by a Joan Baez folk song in the 1970s.

Danbury's lovely setting at the foot of the Sauratown Mountains makes it a good starting point for riding around the famous peak in this area—Hanging Rock. As you start south on NC–8/89, the road climbs and twists around the side of the hills. It levels out a bit after you turn on Mountain Road. You'll feel as

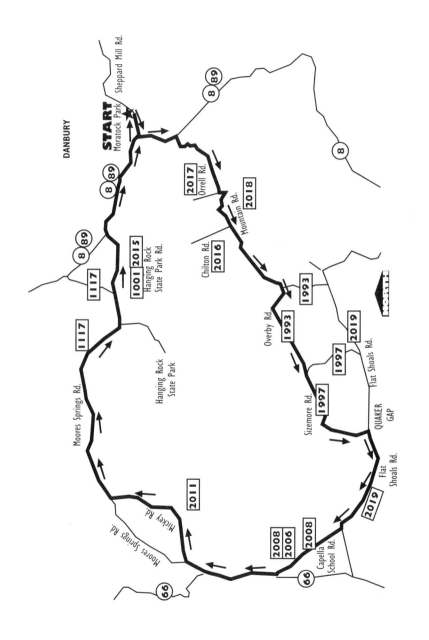

DIREC-TIONS at a glance

0.0 From entrance to Moratock Park (it has a parking lot for your car) in Danbury, turn right onto Sheppard Mill Road.

0.2 Turn left onto NC–8/89, going south.

0.9 Turn right onto Mountain Road (SR 2018).

1.7 Pass Orrell Road on right.

2.7 Pass Chilton Road on right.

4.3 Turn right onto Overby Road (SR 1993).

6.0 Bear right on Sizemore Road (SR 1997).

7.6 Turn right onto Flat Shoals Road (SR 2019).

9.6 Turn right on Capella School Road (SR 2008/2006).

10.6 Turn right onto NC–66.

11.7 Turn right onto Moores Springs Road (SR 1001).

12.1 Turn right onto Mickey Road (SR 2011).

14.0 Turn right onto Moores Springs Road (SR 1001).

17.1 Turn left onto Hanging Rock Park Road (SR 1001/2015). Entrance to park is to the right.

18.6 Turn right onto NC–8/89.

20.5 Turn left onto Sheppard Mill Road.

20.7 Turn left into Moratock Park.

Getting There

From NC–8/89 into Danbury, Moratock Park is on the south side of the downtown area off Sheppard Mill Road about 0.2 miles on the left.

though you've stepped back in time when you see the rustic log house on your right and the old log tobacco barns. In the first mile, you'll have Flat Shoals Mountain on your left. Only a few houses break the forests that stretch along this part of the route. Enjoy the minimal traffic, but watch out for the curves, which aren't always banked correctly for you to take them fast.

The first payoff comes when you reach Sizemore Road and have a great view of Hanging Rock to the right. You can understand how it got its name when you see the masses of rock that appear to be hanging from the side of the mountain.

After you turn on Flat Shoals Road at 7.6 miles, you'll arrive in the small community of Quaker Gap. Straight ahead is Sauratown Mountain, which is easily identified by the transmission towers that grace its summit.

At 10.6 miles you'll turn onto NC–66, which can be very busy at times, so be cautious. It's shady in summer, which can mean that a cyclist is hard to see, especially with the curves. Moores Springs Road at 11.7 miles is a North Carolina Scenic Byway, perfect for cycling. A sign points the way to Hanging Rock Park.

As you study the map and see that you can stay on Moores Springs Road all the way to the park entrance, you may wonder why the directions say to take Mickey Road at 12.1 miles. The big payoff comes on this part of the route. Right after you turn you'll start a climb and there, right in front of you, looms the majestic rocky face of Hanging Rock. This view is one that only the locals are likely to see because it's not visible from the main highways.

In addition to Hanging Rock, you'll have a spectacular view of mountain ridges to your left, separated from you by a broad valley. Enjoy! But also watch for horseback riders who like to frequent this area. At 14.0 miles you again join Moores Springs Road with its smooth surface. The Singletree Inn and Restaurant, located off this road, is known for its big, country breakfasts.

At 17.1 miles the route turns left onto Hanging Rock Park Road. If you'd like more miles and a strenuous challenge, you can take a right here into the park and climb to the lake area. NC–8/89 takes you back into Danbury.

Ride 'Round
Pilot Mountain

Number of miles:	41.7 (44.6 for alternate return)
Approximate pedaling time:	4½ hours
Terrain:	Rolling to hilly
Traffic:	Very light except along NC–67 and NC–268
Things to see:	Pilot Mountain, Pilot Knob, farms, country stores, tobacco barns, Saura-town Mountain
Food:	In East Bend and the town of Pilot Mountain

East Bend in southernmost Surry County, our starting point, has long been a popular destination for area cyclists. It's very common in the warm months to see cyclists lounging on the wooden steps or old benches on the front porch of the country store on Main Street, just across from the town hall, as they cool off while sipping their favorite cold drink. The regulars at the store, long accustomed to seeing us cycling enthusiasts in our strange garb, will nod in greeting and sometimes strike up a conversation.

The area around East Bend makes for relaxing cycling because the peaceful farmland and pastures produce nothing noisier than a mooing cow or a plowing tractor. Fall, spring, and summer bring a profusion of colorful wildflowers along the roads and in pastures, the colors and types changing with the seasons.

At 7.8 miles as you climb Siloam Road (SR 1003), you have some great views of Pilot Mountain as you pass white farm-

houses, neat gardens, and green fields. There's also a tremendous vista of the distant mountains over the nearby hills to your left. You'll wonder what stories the leaning barn and vacant houses could tell about the history of the area and the families that peopled it. Appreciate the relatively new bridge across the Yadkin River at Siloam (at 11.5 miles). The old bridge collapsed many years ago with cars on it, killing a number of people, a major tragedy for this lovely rural area.

Hardy Road (SR 2081) just north of the Yadkin River takes off with a curvy climb before you reach a stretch that presents almost a textbook portfolio of all the variations on white frame farmhouses with front porches, typical of an earlier era. Quaker Church Road (SR 2080) offers an eclectic mix of mobile homes guarded by large satellite dishes interspersed with neat brick ranch houses. At 14.3 miles you cross a small stream, and then the road becomes curvier and the surface turns to tar and gravel for a bit bumpier ride.

Pilot Church Road (SR 2057) displays a grand view of Pilot Knob on the right, and you realize how much closer you are to the mountain. At 17.2 miles an old log tobacco barn and fields of tobacco bear witness to the important role tobacco has played in the North Carolina economy. Along Shoals Road (SR 2048) at 18.3 miles, a colony of purple martin houses illustrates a successful strategy for battling summer insects that bite people and damage crops.

After 20.9 miles, as you enter the town of Pilot Mountain on NC–268, you'll experience a good hill while you share the four lanes with more traffic. This stretch of road is part of North Carolina Bike Route 3. Main Street in Pilot Mountain is a wide street that leads you through downtown, known to Andy Griffith and Mayberry fans as Mount Pilot. On the other side of town, you'll take Old Winston Road (SR 2051) off Old U.S. 52 (SR 1855) for a view of the north side of Pilot Knob, the one most accessible from the major highways. To your left is Sauratown Mountain with its crown of transmission towers.

After you cross U.S. 52 (SR 1855) on Perch Road (SR 1147)

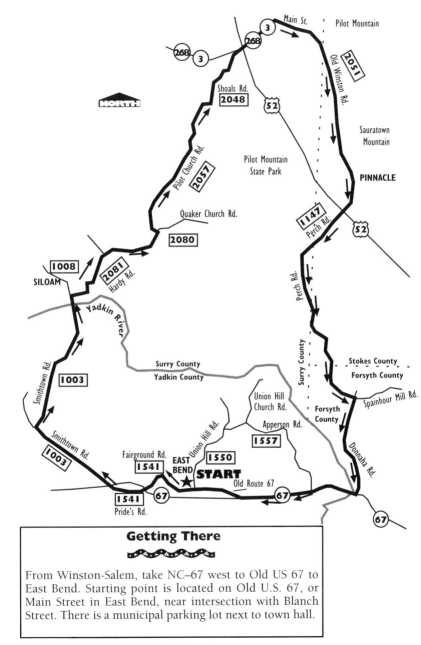

NORTH

268
3
268
3
Main St.
Pilot Mountain
2051
Old Winston Rd.
Shoals Rd.
2048
52
Pilot Church Rd.
2057
Sauratown
Mountain
Pilot Mountain
State Park
PINNACLE
Quaker Church Rd.
2080
1147
Perch Rd.
52
1008
2081
SILOAM
Hardy Rd.
Yadkin River
Perch Rd.
Smithtown Rd.
1003
Surry County
Yadkin County
Surry County
Stokes County
Forsyth County
Union Hill
Church Rd.
Spainhour Mill Rd.
Union Hill Rd.
Apperson Rd.
1557
Forsyth
County
Smithtown Rd.
1003
Fairground Rd.
EAST
BEND
1550
START
Donnaha Rd.
1541
Old Route 67
1541
67
67
67
Pride's Rd.
67

Getting There

From Winston-Salem, take NC–67 west to Old US 67 to
East Bend. Starting point is located on Old U.S. 67, or
Main Street in East Bend, near intersection with Blanch
Street. There is a municipal parking lot next to town hall.

DIREC-TIONS at a glance

0.0 From municipal parking lot in East Bend, next to town hall located at Main Street (Old U.S. 67) and Blanch Street, turn right out of parking lot.

0.2 Turn right onto Fairground Road (SR 1541).

1.1 Cross NC–67; Fairground Road name changes to Pride's Road (SR 1541).

3.3 Turn left onto NC–67, then right onto Smithtown Road (SR 1003).

7.8 Turn right onto Siloam Road (SR 1003).

11.5 Cross Yadkin River into town of Siloam.

11.7 Turn right onto Hardy Road (SR 2081).

13.3 Turn right onto Quaker Church Road (SR 2080).

15.4 Turn left onto Pilot Church Road (SR 2057).

18.3 Turn left onto Shoals Road (SR 2048).

20.9 Turn right onto NC–268 (part of North Carolina Bike Route 3).

22.3 Turn right onto Main Street in town of Pilot Mountain.

23.3 Turn right at yield sign on Old U.S. 52 (SR 1855).

23.4 Turn right onto Old Winston Road (SR 2051).

27.0 Turn right onto Old U.S. 52 (SR 1855) into the town of Pinnacle.

27.4 Turn right onto Perch Road (SR 1147).

28.3 Cross U.S. 52.

32.7 Continue left on Perch Road (SR 1147). Hauser Road goes off to right. As you cross into Forsyth County, the name changes to Spainhour Mill Road.

35.2 Turn right onto Donnaha Rd.

37.7 Turn right on NC–67. (NC–67 is Reynolda Road in Forsyth County.)

41.7 Continue on NC–67 right on Old US 67 into East Bend (Main Street) to parking lot on the right.

Alternate return

39.0 Turn right onto Apperson Road (SR 1557).

40.0 Turn left on Union Hill Church Road.

42.0 Turn left onto Union Hill Road (SR 1550).

44.4 Turn right onto Main Street in East Bend.

44.6 Turn right into parking lot.

---

at 28.3 miles, you'll see the Bear Shoals Canal. Horne Creek Farm, a historical site, is to your right. At 32.7 miles continue left on Perch Road where Hauser Road goes off to the right. This section of road winds its way into Forsyth County with several good climbs and rewarding downhills.

After such a peaceful ride, you may want an alternative to riding the busy NC–67 back to East Bend. The alternate route along Apperson Road is more in keeping with the experiences to this point, although it does add about 3 miles to the distance. When you finish, you'll have crossed parts of four counties in northwestern North Carolina.

Westbend Winery Tour:
Lewisville

Number of miles:	15.7
Approximate pedaling time:	2 hours
Terrain:	Rolling
Traffic:	Light
Things to see:	Vineyards, Westbend Winery, rolling farmland, beautiful homes, forests, a variety of birds and other wildlife
Food:	Food store at The Oaks Shopping Center

Rounding the bend on a rural road in North Carolina and finding acres of well-tended vineyards is something of a surprise. After all, North Carolina has more of a reputation for tobacco and textiles than wine. But Westbend Winery—along with the North Carolina Grape Council—is working hard to change that image. And the peaceful country roads around the vineyards make for fantastic cycling.

This tour starts at a small shopping center in Lewisville that is a popular gathering spot for area cyclists. As the roads closer in to Winston-Salem have grown more congested, cyclists have started meeting here for rides in the western part of Forsyth County and across the Yadkin River into Yadkin and Davie counties.

The only recently paved Williams Road has very little traffic and offers serene, rolling terrain. The attractive homes along the route are interspersed with hardwood forests and small farms. It's not unusual to see bluebirds perched on the numerous fence posts, although mourning doves and robins are much more common.

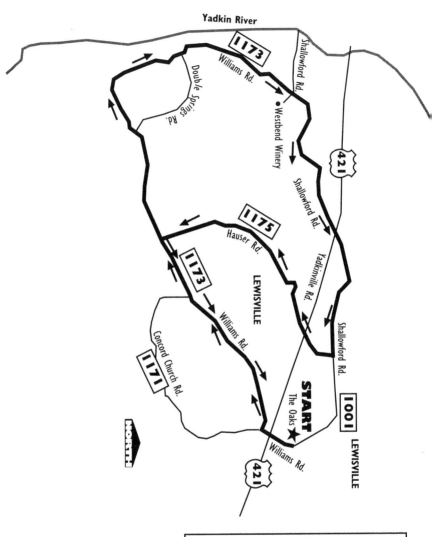

Yadkin River

1173

Shallowford Rd.

Williams Rd.

Double Springs Rd.

• Westbend Winery

Shallowford Rd.

421

1175

Hauser Rd.

Yadkinville Rd.

1173

LEWISVILLE

Williams Rd.

Shallowford Rd.

Concord Church Rd.

1171

1001 LEWISVILLE

START
The Oaks ★

NORTH

Williams Rd.

421

Getting There

From U.S. 421 into Lewisville, turn east onto Concord Church Road. The Oaks Shopping Center is about 0.1 mile on left.

DIRECTIONS at a glance

0.0 From The Oaks Shopping Center, turn right onto Williams Road (SR 1173).

0.3 Turn right onto Williams Road (SR 1173), which shares the exit ramp for U.S. 421, and then left to stay on Williams Road. (You will stay on Williams Road, which has some curves, until you reach Westbend Winery.)

1.7 Pass intersection with Concord Church Road (SR 1171), which goes off to left.

2.3 Pass Hauser Road (SR 1175), which goes off to right.

3.55 Pass Double Springs Road, which goes off to right. A short distance later you pass Double Springs Road once again.

4.31 Turn right into Westbend Winery grounds.

4.56 Enter parking lot for Westbend Winery.

4.8 After your winery tour, turn right onto Williams Road (SR 1173).

6.7 Turn right onto Shallowford Road (SR 1001); Williams Road ends here.

10.25 Turn right onto Hauser Road (SR 1175).

13.0 Turn left onto Williams Road (SR 1173).

15.4 Turn left to stay on Williams Road.

15.7 Turn left into parking lot at The Oaks Shopping Center.

Williams Road runs in front of the winery property, so you'll pass most of the vineyards on your way. Open for visitors on weekend (Friday through Sunday) afternoons, the winery offers guided tours as visitors walk through the actual winery and step out back to see the equipment that's used to harvest the traditional European grape varieties. After the tour, visitors are welcomed to the tasting room, where each of nine wines is opened and tasted in turn. Five of the nine have been awarded gold medals. It's best to mainly taste ad spit to maintain optimum equilibrium on the return trip.

North Carolina's experience with wine goes back to the earliest settlement on Roanoke Island. According to the North Carolina Grape Council, "Sir Walter Raleigh is credited with giving birth to commercial grape production when his men discovered a bronze muscadine vine growing wild." Most of the native North Carolina wines are made from this type of grape. And in the early nineteenth century, North Carolina became the leading wine-producing state in the United States. Prohibition ended wine production in North Carolina as elsewhere. The rebirth of this industry began in 1970.

The first vineyard with traditional European varieties at Westbend was planted in 1972, against the advice of several authorities on agriculture in North Carolina (despite North Carolina's past success with wine). Going against all the odds given by the agricultural experts, the vivifera varieties have thrived on the slopes near the Yadkin River. As the vines flourished, more acreage was planted, which in 1986 produced a seventy-ton harvest. Westbend became a bonded winery in 1988, and the first Westbend wines were released in the summer of 1990.

Williams Road ends at its intersection with Shallowford Road, so named because it crosses the Yadkin River at a shallow point that wagons used to ford. A quick side trip to the river is possible by taking Shallowford Road to the west (turn left at the stop sign before the winery). But be forewarned that the wonderful downhill ride to the river only means a long climb coming back, although a dip in the river may make it all worthwhile.

The route returns through small communities and farmlands along Hauser Road before rejoining Williams Road and heading back to the Oaks.

Old Salem to Bethabara:
Winston-Salem

Number of miles: 17.54
Approximate pedaling time: 3 hours
Terrain: Rolling
Traffic: Light to moderate, except on Reynolda Road, which can be very heavy
Things to see: Historic Old Salem, Historic Bethabara, Reynolda House and Village, Graylyn Estate, historic Broostown Mill, West End neighborhood (historic district), Buena Vista neighborhood, other charming neighborhoods
Food: Restaurants in Old Salem, in West End, along Reynolda and Robinhood Roads

Following this route will give you a wonderful historical perspective on Winston-Salem and this part of the Piedmont of North Carolina. The ride starts in Old Salem, a community established in 1766 when Moravian brethren moved here from Pennsylvania and purchased a large tract of land. Many of the eighteenth-century buildings have been restored or reconstructed according to the Moravians' meticulous records. Costumed guides conduct tours of the historic buildings while others ply trades such as weaving, shoe making, blacksmithing, and baking, much as the original inhabitants must have.

Among the buildings and exhibits to see here are the Single Brothers House, Salem Tavern, Miksch Tobacco Shop, the Museum of Early Southern Decorative Arts, and the Winkler Bakery, the latter of which still produces fresh breads, cookies, and

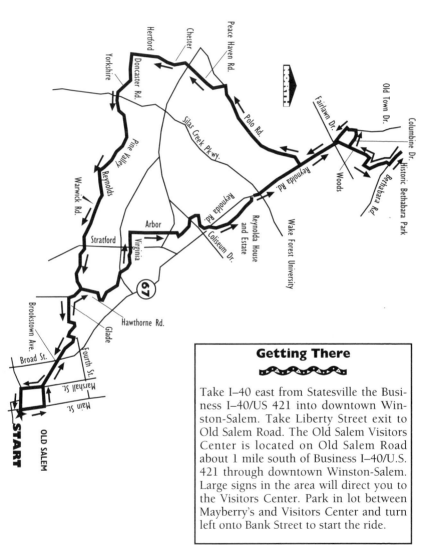

Peace Haven Rd.

Chester

Hertford

Yorkshire

Doncaster Rd.

Old Town Dr.

Fairlawn Dr.

Columbine Dr.

Polo Rd.

Silas Creek Pkwy.

Pine Valley

Reynolda Rd.

Woods

Historic Bethabara Park

Bethabara Rd.

Warwick Rd.

Reynolds

Reynolda Rd.

Wake Forest University

Arbor

Reynolda House and Estate

Coliseum Dr.

Stratford

Virginia

67

Hawthorne Rd.

Brookstown Ave.

Glade

Broad St.

Fourth St.

Marshall St.

Main St.

START

OLD SALEM

Getting There

Take I–40 east from Statesville the Business I–40/US 421 into downtown Winston-Salem. Take Liberty Street exit to Old Salem Road. The Old Salem Visitors Center is located on Old Salem Road about 1 mile south of Business I–40/U.S. 421 through downtown Winston-Salem. Large signs in the area will direct you to the Visitors Center. Park in lot between Mayberry's and Visitors Center and turn left onto Bank Street to start the ride.

**DIREC-
TIONS
at a glance**

0.00 From intersection of Bank and Main Streets (having come up Bank Street after parking in Old Salem Visitors Center parking lot), turn left at stop sign onto Main Street.

0.28 Turn left onto Brookstown Avenue.

0.48 Bear right on Brookstown Avenue (Wachovia Street goes off to left).

0.95 Cross Broad Street.

1.24 Turn left onto Fourth Street.

1.34 Bear right around the park into Glade Street (S curves), then bear left and right around the YWCA, staying on Glade Street.

1.84 Turn right onto Hawthorne Road and cross Northwest Boulevard.

2.04 Bear right on Hawthorne Road after you pass under the railroad trestle (bike route sign points to left, which is the way you'll be returning). Bear right going up hill.

2.30 Turn right into R. J. Reynolds High School. At end of drive (in front of auditorium) is a great view of downtown Winston-Salem. Continue around one-way drive.

2.56 Turn right onto Hawthorne Road at entrance columns.

2.64 Bear left onto Virginia Road.

2.81 Cross Buena Vista Road (pronounced *Bewnah Vihsta* by locals); continue on Virginia Road.

3.12 Cross Stratford Road.

3.34 Turn right onto Arbor Road.

3.84 Cross Robinhood Road.

3.95 Turn left onto Oaklawn Avenue.

4.10 Cross Coliseum Drive into road through Graylyn International Conference Center.

4.19 Bear right toward main building of conference center. Stay on main road until gate at entrance.

4.47 Cross Reynolda Road and go through gates into Reynolda Estate (one-way road).

5.00 At stop sign, turn right to go through Reynolda Village.

5.15 Bear left toward Reynolda Road.

5.21 Turn right onto Reynolda Road.

6.55 Turn right onto Woods Road, immediately after intersection with Fairlawn Drive.

7.19 Turn left onto Old Town Road.

7.43 Turn left onto Bethabara Road (pronounced *buh-THAB-bra*).

7.85 Arrive in Historic Bethabara. For return, reverse direction.

8.21 Turn right onto Old Town Road.

8.46 Turn right onto Woods Road.

8.90 Turn right onto Columbine.

9.18 Turn left onto Old Town Drive.

9.19 Turn left at light onto Reynolda Road.

9.89 Turn right onto Polo Road.

11.31 Turn left onto Peace Haven Road.

11.84 Cross Robinhood Road.

12.34 Turn left on Chester, then immediately bear left on Hertford Road.

12.74 Turn left onto Doncaster Road.

12.94 Turn right onto Yorkshire Road.

13.14 Cross Silas Creek Parkway (steep hill).

13.44 Turn right onto Pine Valley Road.

14.14 Turn left onto Reynolds Drive.

14.44 Bear right onto Warwick Road.

15.14 Cross Stratford Road (Warwick Road changes to Runnymede Road).

15.24 Bear left onto Runnymede Road (bike route).

15.59 Bear right onto Hawthorne Road.

15.64 Cross Northwest Boulevard.

15.84 Turn left onto Glade Street (S curve around the YWCA).

16.34 Bear left onto Fourth Street.

16.44 Turn right onto Brookstown Avenue.

16.74 Cross Broad Street.

17.14 Turn right onto Marshall Street.

17.44 Turn left onto Academy Street.

17.54 Turn right into Old Salem Visitors Center parking lot.

pastries using the original brick ovens. Riding north on Main Street, you'll pass handsome homes built in a variety of styles from the eighteenth and nineteenth centuries, close to the street with tree-lined brick sidewalks.

At about 0.41 miles you pass the Brookstown Mill, which used to produce textiles but is now home to an inn and restaurant. At 1.18 miles you'll see on your right the gazebo for Grace Court Park as you skirt the historic West End, with its elegant houses from the late nineteenth and early twentieth centuries. West End was Winston-Salem's first "suburb," made possible by the trolley service that ran along Fourth Street until well into the 1900s.

As you climb the curving hill on Hawthorne Road at 2.24 miles, turn into the drive for R. J. Reynolds High School—named for the tobacco magnate who founded the company that bears his name. The end of the drive, in front of the wonderful auditorium in the classical style, offers a fantastic view of the downtown skyline and West End. The school nestles in the heart of Buena Vista, one of Winston-Salem's premier neighborhoods.

At 4.04 miles, as you cross Coliseum Drive, you'll enter the Graylyn International Conference Center grounds. The main building as well as the other outbuildings are built with stone in the style of a French château. The estate was built by Bowman Gray and his wife, Nathalie, on land purchased from R. J. Reynolds, whose country estate is across the street. Gray died a short time after the house was finished in the late 1920s, and his family gave the estate to Wake Forest University, which converted it into this elegant conference center.

Across Reynolda Road from Graylyn is Reynolda, Reynolds's country estate, which now is in the midst of the city. The Reynolds heirs, too, gave this estate to Wake Forest University. The estate represented very innovative approaches to farming and self-sufficiency when it was first built. The manor house has since been converted into the Reynolda House Museum of American Art while the farm buildings have been transformed into Reynolda Village, a fascinating complex of shops, restaurants, and offices.

The main entrance to Wake Forest University is located at 5.25 miles and provides an optional side trip. The next point of interest is historic Bethabara, the 1753 site of the first Moravian settlement in the state. The Moravians lived here while they were building Salem. Costumed guides here also conduct tours of the historic buildings. A reconstructed 1756 fort anchors one end of the settlement. Nature and history trails lead visitors to excavation sites.

The return leg of the trip winds through another prime neighborhood called Sherwood Forest and then back through Buena Vista to downtown and Old Salem.

'Round the Lakes Ride:
High Point

Number of miles:	14.5
Approximate pedaling time:	1½ hours
Terrain:	Rolling
Traffic:	Light on side streets, moderate along most main roads, heavy along Skeet Club Road and Eastchester Drive
Things to see:	High Point University campus, Oakview Recreation Center, Oak Hollow marina, Oak Hollow Lake, residential areas of High Point and southern Guilford County
Food:	Restaurants and stores on Hamilton Street, Johnson Street, and Old Greensboro Road

This city got its name by being the "high point" on the original survey for the old North Carolina Railroad. It is known around the world as host twice a year for the International Home Furnishings Market, which swells the area's population by tens of thousands each spring and fall. Of the 125 furniture plants in the area, 15 are among the world's largest. Since much of the industry and traffic are centered in downtown High Point, this tour avoids that congestion by heading north to a more scenic area in the vicinity of Oak Hollow Lake.

The campus of High Point University is our jumping-off point. This main campus attracts primarily traditional students. We'll use the drive through campus to reach West College Avenue at the edge of campus. This first part meanders through older residential sections of town, with stately homes and established trees.

When you turn right on Hamilton Street, which is a one-way street north, you may have to do it without benefit of a street sign. But if you go 1 block too far, you'll run into Johnson Street, which is one way in the opposite direction of the one you want. Hamilton Street merges with Johnson 0.3 mile later to form a busier four-lane street with two-way traffic.

At the intersection with Eastchester Drive, a shopping center on the left offers food and other facilities. This section has a paved shoulder. A short distance later you'll pass the city's water treatment plant and the southernmost tip of Oak Hollow Lake on your right. As you move farther north, the surroundings become more residential and recreational. At 3.9 miles is the Oakview Recreation Center and Oak Hollow Marina. At 4.9 miles you see Oak Hollow Lake on your right, and then the road narrows to two lanes.

Old Mill Road is residential and leads to Waterview Road, which is something of a misnomer except for its far ends. After turning onto Skeet Club Road, you'll cross the northern end of the lake. Skeet Club Road through this part of the county belongs to the Mountains to Sea Bicycle Route, so you may see more cyclists. Braddock Road diverts you from this busy road and offers an optional side trip. At the intersection with Whites Mill Road, you can turn right instead of left for a short trip to Oak Hollow Lake via Oak Hollow Drive.

The trickiest part of the ride comes after you turn onto Eastchester Drive. This busy road has four lanes with a center turn lane. You have 0.4 mile to let the traffic pass so you can negotiate your way into the center turn lane for your left onto Hickswood Road, which wanders through a more rural section, providing a nice interlude before you head back into High Point. A few houses break the stretch of woods. Just after Hickswood Road merges with Deep River Road, you cross the river that gave the road its name. This road eases you back into the urban setting as you approach Greensboro Road and Montlieu Avenue to return to campus.

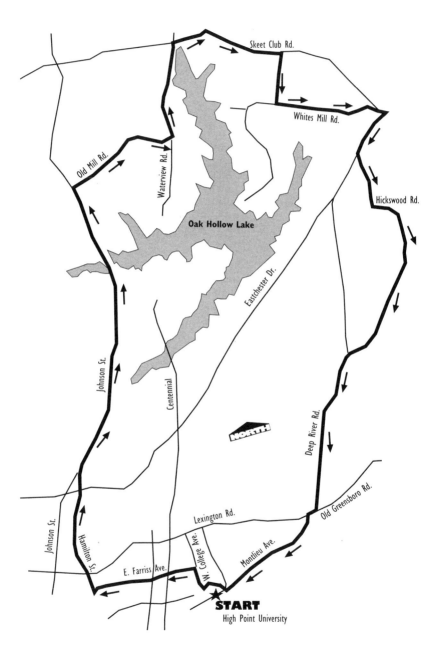

Skeet Club Rd.

Whites Mill Rd.

Old Mill Rd.

Waterview Rd.

Hickswood Rd.

Oak Hollow Lake

Eastchester Dr.

Johnson St.

Centennial

NORTH

Deep River Rd.

Johnson St.

Hamilton St.

Lexington Rd.

Old Greensboro Rd.

E. Farriss Ave.

W. College Ave.

Montlieu Ave.

★ **START**
High Point University

0.0 From the High Point University visitors parking (at the main entrance on Montlieu Avenue) on the traffic circle, bear right on the drive through the college campus.

0.3 Turn right onto West College Avenue.

0.5 Turn left onto East Farriss Avenue. Cross Centennial Street, then jog over at Forrest Street to stay on East Farriss Avenue.

1.7 Turn right onto Hamilton (one-way street north).

2.0 Hamilton merges with Johnson Street (two-way street).

5.4 Turn right onto Old Mill Road.

6.5 Turn left onto Waterview Road.

7.3 Turn right onto Skeet Club Road.

8.3 Turn right onto Braddock Road.

8.7 Turn left onto Whites Mill Road.

9.6 Turn right onto Skeet Club Road.

9.7 Turn right onto Eastchester Drive.

10.1 Turn left onto Hickswood Road.

12.0 Bear left as Hickswood Road merges into Deep River Road.

13.4 Turn right onto Old Greensboro Road.

13.5 Turn left onto Montlieu Avenue.

14.5 Turn right into High Point University visitors parking lot.

Getting There

From either I–40 or I–85, take U.S. 311 (which becomes Main Street) into High Point. Take Montlieu Avenue to the east off Main Street. (Montlieu Avenue is north of the downtown area of High Point.) High Point University is about 1.1 miles on the left off Montlieu Avenue.

GUILFORD
COURT HOUSE
HOBKIRKS HILL
NINETY-SIX
EUTAW SPRINGS

NATHANAEL
APPOINTED MAJOR
COMMAND OF THE
OCTOBER
BORN IN RHODE ISLAND
DIED IN GEORGIA

Air Harbor Tour:
Greensboro

Number of miles:	28.2
Approximate pedaling time:	3 hours
Terrain:	Rolling
Traffic:	Light to moderate
Things to see:	Lake Brandt, Guilford Battleground
Food:	Lots of restaurants along U.S. 220

This route's name comes from the small airport that's located on Air Harbor Road on the route. As you leave the parking lot of the Guilford Courthouse National Military Park, you'll see a wide, paved path adjacent to the road that you may prefer to take if traffic is heavy on Old Battleground Road, as it usually is at rush hour. The bike path ends at Lake Brandt Road, where you turn right.

The first part of the route passes residential developments, which thin out as the route moves farther into the countryside. The two large lakes on the route—Lake Brandt and Lake Townsend—are the principal water supplies for the city of Greensboro.

The principal attraction along the route is the Guilford Courthouse National Military Park at the starting point. Covering about 220 acres, the park memorializes the Revolutionary War battle fought here in March 1781 between General Nathanael Greene's mixed Continental and militia army and the British forces of Lord Cornwallis. Although Cornwallis won the battle, he suffered severe losses and failed to destroy the Revolutionary force. Greene lost the battle but helped force Cornwallis to Virginia, where he finally surrendered at Yorktown in October 1781.

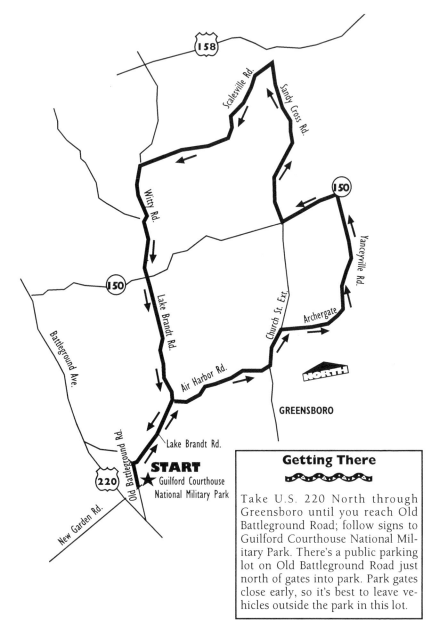

158

Scalesville Rd.

Sandy Cross Rd.

150

Witty Rd.

Yanceyville Rd.

150

Lake Brandt Rd.

Church St. Ext.

Archergate

Battleground Ave.

Air Harbor Rd.

NORTH

GREENSBORO

Old Battleground Rd.

Lake Brandt Rd.

START
★ Guilford Courthouse
National Military Park

220

New Garden Rd.

Getting There

Take U.S. 220 North through Greensboro until you reach Old Battleground Road; follow signs to Guilford Courthouse National Military Park. There's a public parking lot on Old Battleground Road just north of gates into park. Park gates close early, so it's best to leave vehicles outside the park in this lot.

DIRECTIONS at a glance

0.0 From public parking lot on Old Battleground Road just north of gates for Guilford Court-house National Military Park, turn right onto Old Battleground Road.

0.6 Turn right onto Lake Brandt Road.

2.3 Turn right onto Air Harbor Road.

4.85 Turn left onto Church Street.

5.85 Turn right onto Archergate.

6.78 Turn left onto Yanceyville Road.

7.4 Continue on Yanceyville Road.

10.2 Turn left onto NC–150.

11.75 Turn right onto Church Street.

15.59 Turn left onto Scalesville Road.

20.0 Turn left onto Witty Road.

21.4 Turn left onto Lake Brandt Road.

27.25 Turn left onto Old Battleground Road.

28.2 Arrive at public parking lot.

Optional side trip (10 miles)

From Old Battleground Road, take New Garden Road south toward Guilford College. Counting from the intersection of Battleground Avenue and New Garden Road, it's 5 miles to Friendly Avenue. Just before you get to Friendly Avenue (which is a very large intersection), you can turn left into the Guilford College campus. There are many restaurants within walking (or cycling) distance of the college.

The park includes wayside exhibits and markers along a 2.5-mile route. The monuments include those for John Penn and William Hooper, signers of the Declaration of Independence. In the middle of a large grassy area stands the statue of General Greene astride his horse. The Calvary Monument recognizes the contributions of the American cavalry, among them the Goliath of the Revolution, as Peter Francisco of Virginia was known. He is alleged to have wielded a 5-foot sword to protect his massive 260-pound, 6-foot-6-inch body during the battle. The sword was said to have been a gift from General George Washington.

The park itself is a lovely retreat with large expanses of grass and winding trails. It's a popular spot with both cyclists and joggers, especially at the end of the workday and on weekends.

New Garden Road, which ends at Battleground Avenue coming in from the west, offers a nice side trip at the end of the main ride. It leads to Guilford College, the first coeducational institution in the South. Founded by the Quakers in 1837 in the New Garden Community, the school was originally a boarding school aimed at training teachers. Today it serves a wide variety of students seeking a liberal arts education. In the summer it is host to the Eastern Music Festival, a six-week series of recitals, chamber music performances, and symphony concerts presented by guest musicians from around the world and the students who come to study with them for the summer.

Chinqua-Penn
Plantation Tour

Number of miles:	35
Approximate pedaling time:	3 hours
Terrain:	Gently rolling hills
Traffic:	Light
Things to see:	Historic Presbyterian church, Episcopal conference center, farms, Chinqua-Penn Plantation
Food:	Small country store at 13.0 miles, seasonal roadside stand at 27.6 miles

This pleasant ride begins in northern Guilford County (north of Greensboro) and travels into southern Rockingham County to the unique and interesting Chinqua-Penn Plantation, which is open from spring through mid-December each year. The plantation's name derives from the chinquapin tree, a deciduous tree similar to the chestnut.

The rustic log construction of this thirty-room mansion is what makes it unique from an architectural standpoint. But its furnishings and other objects add to the uniqueness. Here you'll see temple altarpieces from Nepal, rare Chinese terra-cotta sculptures, and a fifteenth-century Byzantine mosaic. The extensive grounds and gardens include 30 landscaped acres and an ornate Chinese pagoda. Allow one hour and thirty minutes for the tour. Because of the seasonal hours, it's wise to call ahead before planning your trip.

The area on Wentworth Road is somewhat more densely populated around the plantation, but traffic is still usually light. Even the small country store and roadside stand are rustic and

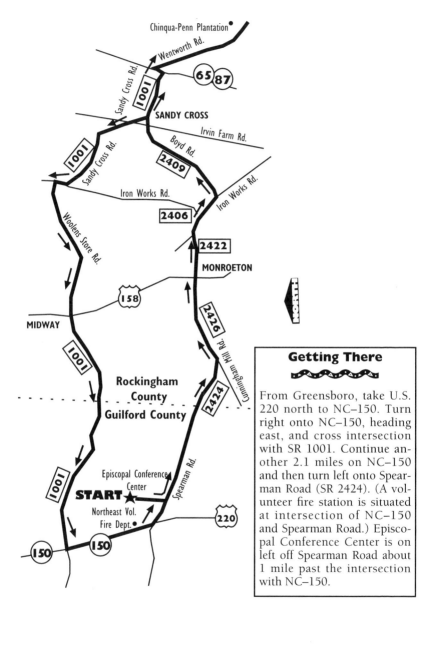

Chinqua-Penn Plantation

Wentworth Rd.

Sandy Cross Rd.

1001

65 87

SANDY CROSS

Irvin Farm Rd.

Boyd Rd.

Sandy Cross Rd.

1001

2409

Iron Works Rd.

Iron Works Rd.

2406

2422

MONROETON

Woolens Store Rd.

158

2426

MIDWAY

Rockingham County

Cunningham Mill Rd.

Guilford County

2424

1001

1001

Episcopal Conference Center

START ★

Spearman Rd.

Northeast Vol. Fire Dept.

220

150

150

Getting There

From Greensboro, take U.S. 220 north to NC–150. Turn right onto NC–150, heading east, and cross intersection with SR 1001. Continue another 2.1 miles on NC–150 and then turn left onto Spearman Road (SR 2424). (A volunteer fire station is situated at intersection of NC–150 and Spearman Road.) Episcopal Conference Center is on left off Spearman Road about 1 mile past the intersection with NC–150.

0.0 From the Summit, the Episcopal Conference Center at Browns Summit, turn left at entrance onto Spearman Road (SR 2424).

1.8 Turn left onto Cunningham Mill Road (SR 2426).

3.5 Stop sign at intersection with Monroeton (U.S. 158); go straight on Monroeton Road (SR 2422).

3.6 Pass Monroeton School (on left just north of U.S. 158).

5.1 Turn right onto SR 2406, which runs into Iron Works Road.

10.5 Turn left onto Boyd Road (SR 2409).

12.9 Cross Irvin Farm Road.

13.0 Country store at intersection with Sandy Cross Road (SR 1001).

14.5 Turn left on NC–65/87. Intersection is offset slightly when you jog left and then turn right onto Wentworth Road

16.5 Turn left into entrance to Chinqua-Penn. After your tour, turn right onto Wentworth Road.

18.5 Turn left on NC–65/87, then right on Sandy Cross Road.

20.0 Bear right at intersection with Boyd Road (SR 2409).

23.8 Turn right onto Iron Works Road. (Watch for upcoming left turn onto SR 1001, which is not clearly marked.)

24.2 Turn left to continue on SR 1001, the name for which becomes Woolens Store Road.

27.6 Roadside stand (seasonal) at intersection of U.S. 158 in Midway. Continue on SR 1001.

31.8 Rumble strips just before SR 1001 runs into NC–150, onto which you turn left.

33.7 Turn left onto Spearman Road (SR 2424).

35.0 Turn left at entrance to Episcopal Conference Center.

fit naturally into the landscape. Most of this route traverses rural areas with neatly maintained farms and small communities. You're likely to see open fields, broken by dense pine and hard-wood forests.

The rolling terrain offers variety and challenge, with descents that carry you past small streams and low-lying wetlands. While the road surfaces are generally smooth and well maintained, they are rather narrow and have many curves. It's wise to position yourself on the roadway so that cars can see you before they are too far into the curve.

A few historic farmhouses dot the countryside along with the old-style log tobacco barns. In the past the tobacco was tied in bundles and hung in these barns for curing. Farmers kept a vigil to be sure the fires were kept burning during the curing process. The cured tobacco was then sold at market.

A historic Presbyterian church organized in 1759 stands by a National Historic site marker that describes a bit of the history. The white-frame building is typical of many churches across the country in rural areas and small towns. Because much of this area was settled by Scottish-Irish immigrants, Presbyterian churches are a common sight in many parts of North Carolina.

The Summit, the Episcopal conference center where the ride begins and ends, hosts religious and secular meetings for groups of up to two hundred people. Nestled in the woods, its grounds include beautiful native plants, walking trails, tennis courts, and a scenic lake with a wooden deck overlooking it all.

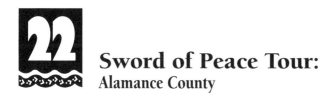

Sword of Peace Tour:
Alamance County

Number of miles:	41.9
Approximate pedaling time:	4 hours
Terrain:	Rolling
Traffic:	Light except on NC–62, which has moderate traffic
Things to see:	Quaker settlement at Snow Camp, outdoor drama *The Sword of Peace*, Alamance Battleground, Alamance County Historical Museum, Cedar Rock Park
Food:	Service station with food and beverages at corner of SR 2351 and SR 1004, restaurant in Snow Camp

Our starting point for this tour is the Alamance Battleground, "Where the Regulators and Militia Met to End the War of Regulation" in the early 1770s. This battlefield, memorialized with an 1880 granite monument, commemorates the struggle of North Carolina Regulators against the abuses and excesses of the government of this British colony under royal governor William Tryon. Tryon's army of less than one thousand men rested on the banks of Alamance Creek before confronting the two thousand Regulators who had assembled 5 miles away.

The two-hour battle resulted in nine fatalities for each side, although the better-equipped and -trained militia also took fifteen prisoners and executed six of them. While the Regulators' efforts at effecting reform were unsuccessful, they demonstrated the high level of discontent among the colonists and foretold the

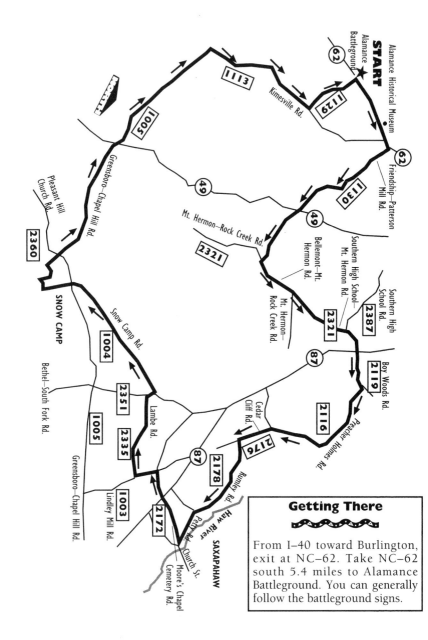

Getting There

From I–40 toward Burlington, exit at NC–62. Take NC–62 south 5.4 miles to Alamance Battleground. You can generally follow the battleground signs.

DIREC-TIONS at a glance

0.0 From parking lot at Alamance Battle-ground, turn left onto NC–62.

1.9 Alamance Historical Museum on left.

2.0 Turn right onto Bike Route 72—Friendship-Patterson Mill Road (SR 1130).

5.2 At stop sign at NC–49; continue straight. Signs for Bike Route 72 and Cedar Rock Park across the highway.

5.5 Cross Cedar Rock Park.

6.9 Turn left at stop sign onto Mt. Hermon–Rock Creek Road (SR 2321), Bike Route 72.

8.5 At stop sign, bear right on Bellemont–Mt. Hermon Road (SR 2321).

8.8 Left on SR 2321, Southern High–Mt. Hermon Road (Bike Route 72 sign).

10.15 At stop sign turn right onto Southern High School Road (SR 2387); follow Bike Route 72. Diagonally across the road is Southern High School.

10.9 At stoplight at intersection with NC–87, go straight following State Bike Route 72. Boy Wood Road (SR 2119), also shown on some signs as Boy Woods, is the road's name on the other side of NC–87.

11.8 Right on Preacher Holmes Road (SR 2116).

14.6 Left on Cedar Cliff Road (SR 2176), following Bike Route 72 signs.

15.4 Left onto Rumley Road (SR 2178), following Bike Route 72 sign.

17.5 Left onto Petty Road (SR 2173), following Bike Route 72 sign.

18.2 Turn left onto Moore's Chapel Cemetery Road, following Bike Route 72 sign into Saxapahaw.

18.35 Intersection with Church Street. Town of Saxapahaw is to the left. Turn back on Moore's Chapel Cemetery Road (SR 2172). Begin Bike Route 72. Stay to left instead of turning right onto Petty Road (SR 2173).

19.35 Continue straight across NC–87.
21.0 At stop sign turn left on Lindley Mill Road (SR 1003).
21.8 Turn right onto Lambe Road (SR 2335).
24.0 Turn right onto Bethel–South Fork Road (SR 2351).
24.2 At stop sign, turn left on Snow Camp Road (SR 1004).
27.4 Go straight across Greensboro–Chapel Hill Road at flashing red light, headed toward Snow Camp.
27.8 Turn right on Sylvan School Road (SR 2360) at the sign about the outdoor drama *The Sword of Peace.*
28.0 Turn right onto Drama Road.
28.5 Turn right on Sylvan School Road (SR 2360).
28.9 Continue straight onto Greensboro–Chapel Hill Road (SR 1005), State Bike Route 2. Pleasant Hill Church goes to left.
32.9 At intersection with NC–49, continue straight across, staying on Greensboro–Chapel Hill Road (SR 1005). Follow Bike Route 2 signs.
36.7 At stop sign turn right on Kimesville Road (SR 1113), beginning State Bike Route 74.(*Note:* SR 1005 and State Bike Route 2 both go left here.)
40.1 Turn left onto Clapp Mill Road (SR 1129).
41.8 Turn right on NC–62. (State Bike Route 2 goes left here.)
41.9 Return to Alamance Battleground Park entrance.

boldness of the colonists and their eventual success during the War of Independence a decade or so later.

The visitors center at the battleground offers an audiovisual presentation of the historical event; a map near the field illustrates the battle and gives a brief history. Also located at the battleground is the Allen House. This log house characterizes those used extensively by frontier settlers in the western part of the colony. According to family sources, the house was probably constructed around 1780 by John Allen and was moved from nearby Snow Camp, then restored and refurbished with its original furnishings. John's sister Amy was married to Hermon Husband, a Quaker and pamphleteer active in the Regulator movement.

Just a short distance from the battleground (at 1.9 miles) is the Alamance County Historical Museum, whose grounds include the Holt family cemetery. The next sight to see along the route comes at Cedar Rock Park, which the route crosses. The road passes through lovely rural areas with scattered houses and farmland broken by clusters of woods. The terrain is rolling, so uphill climbs are rewarded with nice downhill runs.

At 17.85 miles the route takes you into Saxapahaw, across the Buddy Collins Memorial Bridge over the Haw River. The town is built into a hillside overlooking the river and offers an optional side trip for those who are interested in more miles than the route provides. First settled by the Sissipahaw Indians, the town was the site of a pioneer cotton mill built by Quaker John Newlin in 1844 and revived in 1927 by Sellers Manufacturing Company. U.S. Senator B. Everett Jordan from North Carolina had his home here. From Saxapahaw we turn around and head to Snow Camp.

Snow Camp, at 26.25 miles, was founded by the Quakers in 1749. Revolutionary General Cornwallis camped in this area after the Battle of Guilford Courthouse, using the home of Simon Dixon as his headquarters. An outdoor drama, *The Sword of Peace,* recounts the history of the area and the convictions and activities of the Quakers who lived here. At 27.6 miles on Drama Road—a North Carolina Scenic Byway—you can see the log cabins that remain from the Quaker settlement. Ye Olde Country Kitchen Restaurant serves dinner and offers a welcome break. The return loop weaves through the rural countryside and returns you to Alamance Battleground.

Dairyland Loop:
Chapel Hill

Number of miles:	26
Approximate pedaling time:	2¾ hours
Terrain:	Rolling
Traffic:	Greensboro Street can be very busy at peak times
Things to see:	University of North Carolina campus, including the Old Well, Morehead Planetarium, Morehead-Patterson Bell Tower, and Ackland Art Museum; serene rural settings
Food:	Lots of restaurants and eating places on Franklin and Rosemary Streets in Chapel Hill and around Carr Mill Mall in Carrboro; a service station and convenience store in Calvander

This ride starts in downtown Chapel Hill and heads through the adjacent town of Carrboro, a bedroom community for Chapel Hill. On your right as you turn onto North Greensboro Street is Carr Mill, a combination historic site and shopping center. This building, listed on the National Register of Historic Places, was originally the Durham Hosiery Mills in the early twentieth century. The mills' owner Julian S. Carr agreed to provide electricity for the town's 1,000 residents and, in his honor, the town of Venable renamed itself Carrboro. The mills closed during the Depression, making the University of North Carolina the largest employer in the area.

As you leave Carrboro on Hillsborough Road at 2.1 miles, you'll find the houses becoming farther apart, separated by

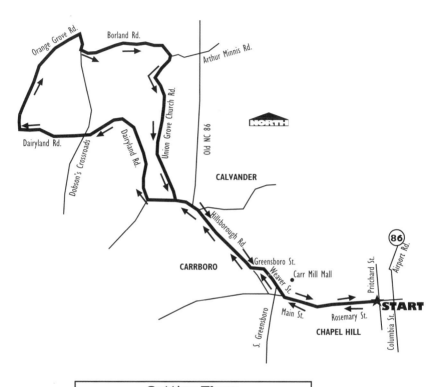

Getting There

From either I–40 or I–85, take NC–86 toward Chapel Hill. As you enter Chapel Hill, NC–86 is called Airport Road, and it merges with Columbia Street. As you reach the intersection with Rosemary Street, you'll see one public parking lot to your left across Rosemary Street. The other is 1 block west (to your right) on Rosemary.

DIREC-TIONS at a glance

0.0 From intersection of Rosemary and Pritchard Streets in Chapel Hill, turn left onto Rosemary Street, going west.

0.5 Rosemary Street becomes Main Street in Carrboro.

0.7 Turn right onto Weaver Street (Carr Mill Mall on right).

0.8 Turn right onto Greensboro Street, which has bike lanes.

2.1 Bear right onto Hillsborough Road when Greensboro Street ends.

4.1 Turn left onto Dairyland Road in Calvander. Old NC–86 goes off to the right. (Intersection can be a bit confusing because of the number of roads at intersection.)

10.9 Turn right onto Orange Grove Road.

14.1 Turn right onto Dobson's Crossroads.

14.5 Turn left onto Borland Road (curvy road).

17.3 Turn right onto Arthur Minnis Road.

17.9 Turn left onto Union Grove Church Road.

21.3 Turn left onto Dairyland Road.

21.9 Turn right onto Hillsborough Road in Calvander.

22.6 Bear left on Hillsborough Road.

23.9 Bear left onto Greensboro Street.

25.1 Turn left onto Weaver Street.

25.25 Bear left onto Main Street in Carrboro.

25.4 Bear left onto Rosemary Street in Chapel Hill.

26.0 Turn right into parking lot.

golden fields of grain with a few new housing developments. One of these new developments, called Arcadia, to the north of town provides an innovative housing model concentrating on sustainable, energy-efficient environment using active and passive solar features in its buildings.

In the crossroads community of Calvander at 4.1 miles, you'll take Dairyland Road, which gets its name from the many dairy farms that grace this part of the county. Pristine white fences, expansive fields of corn, rolling hills, and grazing cattle characterize this part of the ride. In some places you can see remnants of damage from Hurricane Fran, which hit the area in September 1996, uprooting many large trees and wreaking devastation on the Triangle, the name for the Chapel Hill–Durham–Raleigh section of the state.

On Orange Grove Road at 10.9 miles, you'll see Possum's Country Store, a sample of the colorful names given to roads and businesses in rural North Carolina. Borland Road at 14.5 miles offers lots of curves, so be sure to ride far enough into the lane that cars approaching the curve can see you in time.

You'll want to save some time—at either the beginning or the end of your ride—to visit the sights in Chapel Hill. Franklin Street, which is parallel to Rosemary Street 1 block south, is the main street in this lovely historic town. Lots of interesting shops and restaurants line Chapel Hill's streets, which are busy year-round with university students and staff. The Morehead Planetarium on East Franklin Street just east of Columbia Street is part of the University of North Carolina and contains a walk-in model of the solar system. Planetarium shows are presented evenings and for weekend matinees.

The Ackland Art Museum, just south of Franklin Street on Columbia Street, offers displays of paintings, drawings, sculptures, and other artworks representing Oriental, classical, twentieth-century, and North Carolina folk art.

The University of North Carolina, chartered in 1789, is one of the oldest state-chartered universities in the United States and was the first to accept and graduate students. The Old Well, a symbol of the university, can be found by walking through the campus behind the Morehead Planetarium. Parking is limited on campus, so biking and walking are the preferred modes of transportation here.

24 Duke Forest Ride:
Durham

Number of miles:	29.4
Approximate pedaling time:	2½ hours
Terrain:	Rolling
Traffic:	Light on secondary roads, moderate on Hillsborough Road, heavy on NC–86.
Things to see:	Bennett Place State Historic Site, parts of Duke Forest
Food:	Service station with convenience store in Calvander

Bennett Place marks the location of the surrender that ended the Civil War on April 26, 1865, for Florida, Georgia, and the Carolinas, seventeen days after General Robert E. Lee's surrender at Appomattox, Virginia. Here General Joseph E. Johnston surrendered most of the remaining Confederate army remaining in the field. The triumphant Union general was William Tecumseh Sherman, who had just completed his march to the sea. Each April a reenactment ceremony retells this historic event.

The original home burned in 1921, and a replica was built in 1961. The site now includes the restored homestead and a visitors center where you can see exhibits on North Carolina's role in the Civil War, along with photographs, flags, guns, and uniforms. An audiovisual presentation is available on request, as are guided tours. The shady grounds offer picnic facilities.

You'll exit Bennett Place on Bennett Memorial Road. This road, thankfully short, is narrow with rough pavement. You'll cross a broad valley before turning left onto New Hope Church

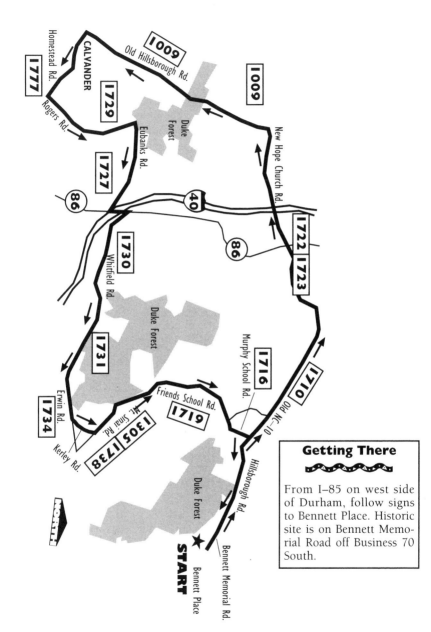

1009

1777
Homestead Rd.
CALVANDER
Old Hillsborough Rd.
1729
1009
Rogers Rd.
Duke Forest
New Hope Church Rd.
Eubanks Rd.
1727
86
40
86
1722 1723
1730
Whitfield Rd.
Duke Forest
Murphy School Rd.
1716
1710 Old NC-10
1731
Erwin Rd.
Friends School Rd.
Mt. Sinai Rd.
1734
Kerley Rd.
1305 1738
1719
Duke Forest
Hillsborough Rd.
START
Bennett Place
Bennett Memorial Rd.

Getting There

From I–85 on west side of Durham, follow signs to Bennett Place. Historic site is on Bennett Memorial Road off Business 70 South.

0.0 From parking lot at Bennett Place State Historic Site, turn left onto Bennett Memorial Road.

0.5 Turn left onto Hillsborough Road (Old U.S. 70).

0.8 Turn left onto SR 1710/Old NC–10.

4.6 Turn left onto New Hope Church Road (no sign with name; SR 1722 or 1723).

8.9 Turn left onto Old NC–86 (SR 1009; also called Old Hillsborough Road).

12.9 Turn left onto Homestead Road (SR 1777).

15.0 Turn left onto Rogers Road (SR 1729).

16.3 Turn right onto Eubanks Road (SR 1727).

18.0 Turn left onto NC–86.

18.3 Turn right onto Whitfield Road (SR 1730, which becomes SR 1731).

21.8 Turn left onto Erwin Road (SR 1734).

22.8 Turn left onto Kerley Road (SR 1304).

23.1 Turn left onto Mt. Sinai Road (SR 1305/1718).

24.8 Turn right onto Friends School Road (SR 1719).

26.1 Turn right onto Murphy School Road (SR 1716; no sign with name).

27.1 Turn right onto Old NC–10 (SR 1710; no sign with name).

28.6 Turn right onto Hillsborough Road (Old U.S. 70).

28.85 Bear right onto Bennett Memorial Road.

29.4 Turn right into Bennett Place.

Road. Watch the signs carefully because they don't agree—one says SR 1722 while another says SR 1723. In some places the names of the roads are missing from the signs, but you can usually rely on the SR numbers. Old U.S. 86 is a winding road with a nice surface but no shoulders.

Mt. Sinai Road and Whitfield Road skirt one section of Duke Forest (Korstian Division). This section contains over one thousand acres of wildlife and forest preserve. Over 10 miles of improved dirt roads and fire trails offer many hiking and biking opportunities. New Hope Creek flows east through the forest, providing numerous side trails and secluded picnic spots. Fishing, swimming, and kayaking in New Hope Creek are possible, depending on seasonal water flow variations.

The beauty of this area was first chronicled by John Lawson in 1701, who called it the "flower of the Carolinas." Before the Europeans came, two Native American tribes—the Eno and the Occoneechi—lived and farmed here. Durham is believed to be the site for an ancient village named Adshusheer. During the mid-1700s, Scottish, Irish, and British immigrants settled in the area on land granted by King Charles I—for whom the Carolinas are named—to John Carteret, earl of Granville.

Nearby, Duke University is situated on the west side of Durham. With its outstanding Gothic architecture, the campus is well worth seeing. Founded originally as Trinity College in Randolph County, the college moved to Durham at the end of the nineteenth century, thanks to Washington Duke and Julian Carr, who donated the land and the money for the move. The school was renamed Duke University after James Buchanan Duke, son of Washington Duke, who donated $40 million to the university.

Historic Tour of Raleigh

Number of miles:	6.3
Approximate pedaling time:	1 hour
Terrain:	Mostly flat
Traffic:	Light on side streets to heavy on main streets in downtown area on weekdays; on weekends downtown streets are virtually deserted
Things to see:	St. Mary's campus, the Joel Lane House, the State Capitol Building, large acorn sculpture, stately homes in Oakwood Historic District, St. Augustine's College, Peace College, Governor's Mansion, North Carolina Legislative Building, North Carolina Museum of History, North Carolina Museum of Natural History
Food:	Restaurants and convenience stores all along route

Named for Sir Walter Raleigh, this state capital city is relatively friendly to cyclists. Our route circles through some of the most interesting sights in the center city, which retains much charm and belies the rapid growth of Wake County outside the beltway.

St. Mary's, our starting point, is an Episcopal school for girls that was established in 1842 by Rev. Albert Smedes on the site of an earlier school for boys. At the edge of St. Mary's campus is the site of the Joel Lane House, which was built before 1770 and was the meeting place where it was decided to locate the town of Raleigh on Lane's land in 1792.

Hillsborough Street leads directly to the State Capitol Building. The capitol, standing majestically on Capitol Square, has been restored to its neoclassical splendor. Under construction from 1833 to 1840, the building is open for tours and now houses the governor's office and other executive functions.

On Martin Street, after you cross Blount Street at 1.1 miles, you'll see Moore Square Park on your left with its huge acorn sculpture paying tribute to the mighty oak trees that surround it. The City Cemetery on East Street (at 1.5 miles) was established in 1798.

You enter the Historic District of Oakwood after you turn right on Jones Street at 1.9 miles. This elegant turn-of-the-century community was declining rapidly when visionary Raleigh residents formed a preservation group to encourage families to move in and restore these charming homes. This street is also part of Raleigh Bike Route 9.

St. Augustine's College, on Oakwood Street at 2.9 miles, is one of the earliest black colleges in the South, and it continued to produce educated and talented alumni, even during the dark days of the Jim Crow era. Among its most famous alumni were the Delany sisters, one an educator and the other a dentist, both of whom lived to be over one hundred years old. They told their lively and interesting story in the bestseller *Having Our Say.*

As you go east on Oakwood, you pass the Oakwood Cemetery and reenter the Historic Oakwood District. Where Boundary Street ends at Person Street (at 4.2 miles), you face a dilemma because you need to go south on Person but it's a one-way street to the north. You can take advantage of being a cyclist by cutting through the Krispy Kreme parking lot and perhaps stopping in for a sugary treat. Krispy Kreme doughnuts were born in North Carolina and are now a favorite of people up and down the East Coast.

As you exit Krispy Kreme, turn right onto Peace Street so you can circle Peace College. This Presbyterian school, founded in 1857, hosted a Confederate hospital in its main building during the Civil War. Blount Street runs south by large old homes, including the Governor's Mansion on the left at the intersection

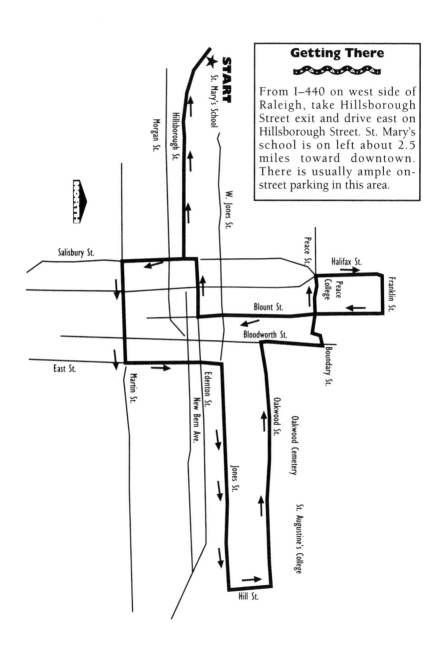

START
St. Mary's School

Getting There

From I–440 on west side of Raleigh, take Hillsborough Street exit and drive east on Hillsborough Street. St. Mary's school is on left about 2.5 miles toward downtown. There is usually ample on-street parking in this area.

NORTH

Morgan St.

Hillsborough St.

W. Jones St.

Salisbury St.

Peace St.

Halifax St.

Peace College

Franklin St.

Blount St.

Bloodworth St.

Boundary St.

East St.

Martin St.

Edenton St.

New Bern Ave.

Jones St.

Oakwood St.

Oakwood Cemetery

St. Augustine's College

Hill St.

DIREC-TIONS at a glance

0.0 From main entrance to St. Mary's school on Hillsborough Street, turn left onto Hillsborough Street and head east toward downtown Raleigh.

0.8 Turn right onto Salisbury Street.

1.1 Turn left onto Martin Street.

1.5 Turn left onto East Street.

1.9 Turn right onto Jones Street.

2.7 Turn left onto Hill Street.

2.9 Turn left onto Oakwood Street.

3.9 Turn right onto Bloodworth Street.

4.1 Turn left onto Boundary Street.

4.2 At Person Street, which is a one-way street north, cut left through the Krispy Kreme Doughnut parking lot to Peace Street.

4.3 Turn right onto Peace Street.

4.5 Turn right onto Halifax Street.

4.6 Turn right onto Franklin Street.

4.7 Turn right onto Blount Street.

5.3 Turn right onto Edenton Street (one-way street west).

5.5 Turn left onto Salisbury Street.

5.6 Turn right onto Hillsborough Street.

6.3 Turn right at entrance to St. Mary's school.

with Jones Street, with its unusual Victorian architecture.

The North Carolina Legislative Building, designed by renowned architect Edward Durrell Stone, presents its colonnaded, marble face to the south. Its dramatic styling includes exterior roof gardens that adorn the upper reaches of the building, which rises from a 340-foot-wide podium of North Carolina granite. The state seal set in terrazzo, 28 feet in diameter, welcomes visitors and legislators to the main entrance.

On Edenton Street at 5.3 miles are the North Carolina Museums of Natural History and History, which also merit a visit.

North Carolina State University Tour:
Raleigh

Number of miles:	13.1
Approximate pedaling time:	1¼ hours
Terrain:	Rolling to hilly in places
Traffic:	Relatively light, although the route does cross some very busy thoroughfares
Things to see:	Campus of North Carolina State University, residential neighborhoods near campus, North Carolina State Fairgrounds, part of NCSU Centennial Campus, NCSU Veterinary College
Food:	Along Hillsborough Street, along Western Boulevard; some campus facilities may be open, particularly the Witherspoon Student Center

This tour wends through the western side of the North Carolina State University (NCSU) campus and surrounding neighborhoods. Established as a land-grant agricultural college, the university—now part of the University of North Carolina system—offers a multitude of undergraduate and graduate degrees, although it is probably still best known for its engineering and design programs. Part of this route includes Raleigh Bike Route 7, so you'll see those signs along the way.

The contemporary Witherspoon Student Center Building, located on Dan Allen Drive on your left, offers rest rooms and food, although its hours vary with the academic calendar.

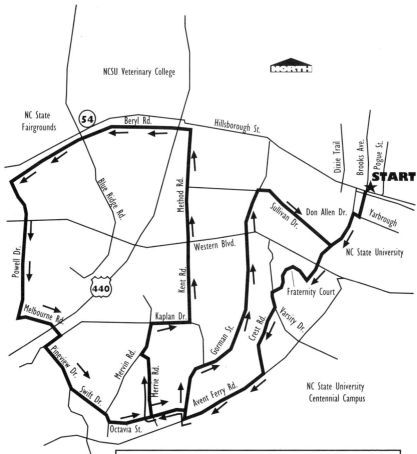

NCSU Veterinary College

NORTH

NC State Fairgrounds

54 Beryl Rd.

Hillsborough St.

Dixie Trail

Brooks Ave.

Pogue St.

START

Blue Ridge Rd.

Method Rd.

Sullivan Dr.

Don Allen Dr.

Yarbrough

NC State University

Powell Dr.

Western Blvd.

440

Kent Rd.

Fraternity Court

Melbourne Rd.

Kaplan Dr.

Gorman St.

Crest Rd.

Varsity Dr.

Pineview Dr.

Mervin Rd.

Merrie Rd.

NC State University Centennial Campus

Swift Dr.

Avent Ferry Rd.

Octavia St.

Getting There

From I–440 on west side of Raleigh, take Hillsborough Street exit and drive east on Hillsborough Street. North Carolina State University is on your right about 1 mile toward downtown. Brooks Street intersects with Hillsborough Street near main entrance to campus. There is usually on-street parking on the access street that parallels Hillsborough Street and on the cross streets of Dixie Trail and Pogue Street.

0.0 From the intersection of Hillsborough Street and Brooks Avenue, head south on Brooks Avenue to ride through the North Carolina State University campus.

0.1 Turn right onto Yarbrough, then left onto Dan Allen Drive.

0.4 Cross Western Boulevard.

0.6 Turn right onto Fraternity Court.

1.1 Turn left onto Varsity Drive.

1.2 Turn right onto Crest Road.

1.6 Turn right onto Avent Ferry Road.

2.1 Turn right onto Gorman Street, then left onto Octavia Street (part of Raleigh's Bike Route 5).

2.3 Turn right onto Merrie Road.

2.7 Turn right onto Mervin Road.

2.9 Turn right onto Kaplan Drive.

3.1 Turn left onto Kent Road (no sign, but Kaplan Square is on left).

3.6 Cross Western Boulevard. Kent Road name changes to Method Road.

4.8 Turn left onto Beryl Road.

5.8 Continue straight across Blue Ridge Road (tricky intersection).

7.1 Turn left onto Powell Drive.

7.4 Cross Western Boulevard.

8.0 Turn left onto Melbourne Road.

8.3 Turn right onto Kaplan Drive.

8.4 Turn left onto Pineview Drive.

8.7 Bear left onto Swift Drive.

9.0 Turn left onto Octavia Street.

9.5 Turn left onto Gorman Street.

10.7 Cross Western Boulevard one last time.

12.2 Turn right onto Sullivan Drive.

12.8 Turn left onto Dan Allen Drive.

13.0 Turn right onto Yarbrough Drive.

13.1 Turn left onto Brooks Avenue and return to starting point.

After you cross Western Boulevard—which you'll crisscross several more times—you'll arrive at Fraternity Court at 0.6 miles. Varsity Drive at 1.1 miles leads toward the Centennial Campus, which you'll see off to your left in the distance as you turn right on Crest Road. That could also make an interesting side trip. Merrie Road at 2.3 miles introduces some hills into your ride for extra challenge. The turn onto Kent Road is tricky because there may not be a street sign there. Just look for Kaplan Square complex on your left.

After you again cross Western Boulevard at 3.6 miles, Kent Road's name changes to Method Road and the NCSU campus is on your right. Beryl Road takes you past the Horticultural Center and the Arboretum. Looking across Hillsborough Street to your right, you can see the NCSU Veterinary College and then the North Carolina State Fairgrounds. The intersection with Blue Ridge Road is tricky because it is wide and railroad tracks run between Beryl Road and Hillsborough, so there's the potential for train movement to back up motor vehicle traffic. Fortunately the train runs are not frequent.

The tour outside the campus visits samples of every type of residential area present in Raleigh—from large stately homes to small bungalows, apartments, and condominiums, and from large forested lots to small tracts. You'll quickly see why Raleigh is known as the City of Oaks, although Hurricane Fran in September 1996 destroyed many of the city's trees. Raleigh's citizens have been active in preservation of natural areas throughout the city.

Gorman Street at 9.5 miles, part of Raleigh Bike Route 5, is a wide two-lane street that leads back to the starting point on campus. As you turn on Brooks Avenue, you'll see some of the university greenhouses to your right.

If you're interested in extending this route, you can follow Avent Ferry Road (Raleigh Bike Route 7) to its terminus at Lake Johnson Park. Another option is to take Yarbrough Drive east to Pullen Park adjacent to the NCSU campus. The park has many attractions for children, including a 1911 Dentzel carousel. Gorman Street (Raleigh Bike Route 5) connects at its south end with

Raleigh Bike Route 6, which crosses southern Raleigh from west to east.

Raleigh also has created a system of public recreational trails and greenways covering 34 miles. You can find out more by calling the Greater Raleigh Convention and Visitors Bureau at (800) 849–8499.

27

House in the Horseshoe Ride:
Moore County

Number of miles:	20.9
Approximate pedaling time:	2 hours
Terrain:	Rolling, with a few good climbs
Traffic:	Light to moderate
Things to see:	Pine forests, pastures, House in the Horseshoe Historic Site
Food:	In Carthage; vending machines at Alston House

This ride offers a firsthand look at longleaf pine forests in Moore County in the Sandhills region of North Carolina. This area is recognized as one of the last remaining strongholds of longleaf pine in the entire southeastern United States. This pine, which was once the dominant tree throughout the Southeast from Virginia to Texas, covering approximately 92 million acres, is recognizable by its long needles—up to 15 inches in length—and its long, narrow cones, which range from 6 to 10 inches.

The region takes its name from the rolling hills topped with deep coarse sands that dominate the landscape and clearly differ from the red clay of the Piedmont area of the state. It is now believed that sediment-filled rivers millions of years ago formed a delta in this area where the rivers flowed into the sea. Over a span of forty to fifty million years, erosion from sandy winds and streams carved the hilly terrain.

Despite a harsh, desertlike environment, an amazing variety of plant and animal life flourishes here. And fire has played an important role in the life cycles of certain animals and plants. It is thought that summer lightning or Native American burning practices caused fire to sweep across vast areas about every two to seven years. Some plants such as the longleaf pine and the abundant wire grass depend on the periodic fires for their reproduction.

Look for other wildlife such as deer and fox squirrels as you ride along the smooth surface of Glendon-Carthage Road (SR 1006). Besides the forests, you'll pass farmlands and open, rolling pastures broken only by small stands of trees and clumps of low-growing shrubs. This part of the route takes you up and down the rolling countryside.

At 7.5 miles you'll bear right onto South Carbottom Road (SR 1621), even though one of the Moore County bike routes follows SR 1006 Glendon–Carthage Road to the left. About 2.5 miles later you'll see a sign for the Alston House, also known as the House in the Horseshoe. The house itself, about half a mile down this road, was so named because it is situated on a hilltop in the horseshoe bend of the Deep River. The elegant house, built in 1772, was home to Philip Alston, a colonel in the Whig or Revolutionary Army.

During the American Revolution the backcountry of North Carolina was the site of periodic battles between groups of citizen-soldiers who were either revolutionaries (Whigs) or loyalists (Tories). On the morning of August 5, 1781, Alston and his revolutionary comrades were camped at his house when they were attacked by a larger unit of Tories. The numerous bullet holes in both the front and back of the house still bear witness to the battle. Fortunately, Mrs. Alston and her children were sheltered in one of the large fireplaces in the house to protect themselves from the bullets. During the battle the Tories tried to set fire to the house by rolling a cart filled with burning straw against its wall. Seeing himself outnumbered and wanting to prevent the destruction of his lovely home, Alston surrendered. In 1790 he sold the house and plantation and left the state.

The house and 2,500-acre plantation were bought in 1798 by Governor Benjamin Williams, who called the estate his "Re-

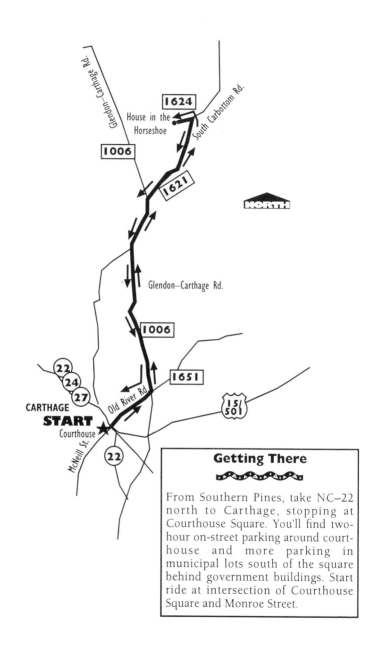

1624

House in the
Horseshoe

South Carbottom Rd.

Glendon–Carthage Rd.

1006

1621

NORTH

Glendon–Carthage Rd.

1006

22
24
27

CARTHAGE
START
Courthouse

1651

Old River Rd.

15
501

McNeill St.

22

Getting There

From Southern Pines, take NC–22
north to Carthage, stopping at
Courthouse Square. You'll find two-
hour on-street parking around courthouse and more parking in
municipal lots south of the square
behind government buildings. Start
ride at intersection of Courthouse
Square and Monroe Street.

DIREC- TIONS
at a glance

0.0 From Courthouse Square at Monroe Street in Carthage, turn right onto Monroe Street.

0.1 Turn left onto McNeill, which becomes Summit Street and then Old River Road (SR 1651).

1.6 Turn left onto Glendon–Carthage Road (SR 1006).

7.5 Turn right onto South Carbottom Road (SR 1621). Glendon–Carthage Road (SR 1006) veers off to left.

10.0 Turn left onto SR 1624 to Alston House—the House in the Horseshoe.

10.5 Arrive at house. After your visit, exit by turning right onto SR 1624.

11.0 Turn right onto South Carbottom Road (SR 1621).

13.5 Turn left onto Glendon–Carthage Road (SR 1006).

19.4 Turn right onto Old River Road (SR 1651), which becomes Summit Street and then McNeill Street.

20.9 Turn right onto Monroe Street to Courthouse Square.

treat." He had served as governor of North Carolina, as a captain under George Washington, as a member of the first board of trustees of the University of North Carolina, and as a member of the National Congress in Philadelphia.

Pottery Loop:
Moore County

Number of miles:	35.1
Approximate pedaling time:	3½ hours
Terrain:	Rolling, with some good climbs
Traffic:	Light
Things to see:	Beautiful farms, family-owned potteries and shops
Food:	In Robbins; otherwise some vending machines at potteries

The northwestern part of Moore County is noted for the number and variety of potters who live and work in the area. Many are descendants of the English settlers, themselves potters by trade, who were attracted to this area by the abundance of clay. Although pottery was produced in the area as early as 1750, it gained popularity as a trade only during Reconstruction after the Civil War. At that time the economy had collapsed and farmers could not market their crops, so many began making and selling whiskey jugs. Prohibition greatly reduced demand for the whiskey jugs, but interest in pottery as an American craft has seen a resurgence in the industry in the last decade or so.

Jugtown Pottery, where the tour begins, is one of the better-known potteries in the area. Various different clay items are on display and for sale in the cozy cabin shop where visitors are welcomed. You can pick up a map of other area potteries if you're interested in more than those along the tour.

You start on Busbee Road (SR 1419) and, just after you cross SR 1003, you'll see Southern Folk Pottery on your right. Howard Mill Road (SR 1456) takes you on rolling hills through fertile farmlands. After you cross the river at 5.1 miles, you turn right

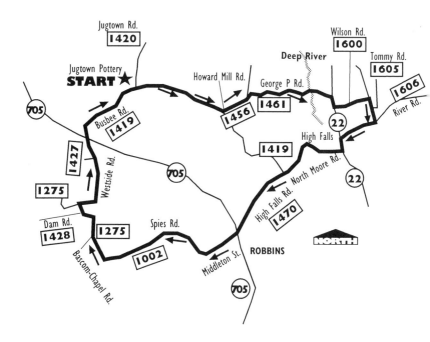

Jugtown Rd.
1420

Jugtown Pottery
START ★

Jugtown Pottery
Busbee Rd.
1419

705

Westside Rd.

1427

1275

Dam Rd.
1428

Bascom-Chapel Rd.

1275

Spies Rd.

1002

Middleton St.

705

Howard Mill Rd.

George P Rd.

Deep River

Wilson Rd.
1600

Tommy Rd.
1605

1606

River Rd.

1456

1461

22

High Falls

1419

North Moore Rd.

High Falls Rd.

1470

22

ROBBINS

NORTH

Getting There

From U.S. 220 in Seagrove, take NC–705 into Moore County. Turn left onto Busbee Road (SR 1419) and then left onto Jugtown Road (SR 1420). Follow signs to Jugtown Pottery.

DIREC-TIONS at a glance

0.0 From Jugtown Pottery on Jugtown Road (SR 1420), turn right onto SR 1420.
0.1 Turn left onto Busbee Road (SR 1419).
0.7 Continue straight across SR 1003.
4.2 Turn left onto Howard Mill Road (SR 1456).
6.1 Turn right onto George P Road (SR 1461).
9.4 Turn right onto NC–22.
9.8 Turn left onto Wilson Road (SR 1600).
11.1 Turn right onto Tommy Road (SR 1605). SR 1603 goes to the left.
11.6 Turn right at stop sign to stay on SR 1605.
12.1 Turn right onto River Road (SR 1606).
13.6 Turn left onto NC–22.
14.0 Turn right onto North Moore Road (SR 1470).
16.1 At intersection with SR 1419, continue on SR 1470, the name for which becomes High Falls Road.
18.7 In Robbins, High Falls Road becomes Middleton Street but remains SR 1470. After crossing NC–705, SR 1470 becomes SR 1002 but remains Middleton Street. SR 1002 soon after becomes Spies Road.
23.0 Turn right on SR 1002.
27.1 Turn right onto Bascom-Chapel Road (SR 1275).
29.3 Turn right onto Dam Road (SR 1428).
31.6 Turn left onto Westside Road (SR 1427).
32.3 Turn left onto NC–705.
32.5 Turn right onto Busbee Road (SR 1419).
35.0 Turn left onto Jugtown Road (SR 1420).
35.1 Turn left into Jugtown Pottery.

on George P Road (SR 1461), which presents some challenging hills through the woods and farmland. Chicken and dairy farms line the road, their pastures spotted with small farm ponds. At 12.1 miles River Road (SR 1606) leads you toward the community of High Falls. NC–22 leads you across the river before you turn right on North Moore Road (SR 1470). You'll see a small lake along this road as well as North Moore High School.

SR 1470 becomes High Falls Road toward Robbins, and then it becomes Middleton Street (SR 1002) after you cross the intersection with NC–705. Outside of town it becomes Spies Road and offers a good downhill till you cross Cabin Creek. A rest area is available off the left of Westside Road (SR 1427) at 31.6 miles.

The preponderance of potteries on this tour are located along Busbee Road (after 32.5 miles). Look for the signs for Westmoore Pottery, Millcreek Forge, Hickory Hill Pottery, 7 Springs Farm, O'Quinn Pottery, Yadkin Trail Pottery and Leather, Cady Clay Works, and Owens Pottery. The latter, which has been in business for over a century, since 1895, has produced the work of the Ben Owen family. Another member of the family, Ben Owen, and his descendants produce clay designs that are well known and exhibited in such places as the Smithsonian.

You'll see a sign for Scott's Pottery as you turn onto Jugtown Road (SR 1420), and more are situated farther down that road past Jugtown Pottery. If you're still in the mood for riding, you would do well to explore more of this area. But be forewarned—you might want to bring panniers or backpacks to haul back the lovely clay pieces that will tempt you.

Pedaling to Pinehurst:
Moore County

Number of miles:	16.8
Approximate pedaling time:	1½ hours
Terrain:	Rolling
Traffic:	Light on side streets to moderate on NC–2
Things to see:	Pinehurst Hotel, village of Pinehurst, quaint shops, elegant homes
Food:	In Southern Pines and Pinehurst

If you had no idea you were in the middle of golf country, you might figure it out on this tour. As you pedal from Southern Pines to Pinehurst, the route takes you past some of the most prestigious golf resorts in the Southeast.

As you leave Southern Pines, you'll take Broad Street until Vermont Road, cross the railroad tracks, and then go right onto Northwest Broad Street, where the street becomes two-way again. At Delaware Street the road divides into four lanes with trees in the middle and Northwest Broad Street becomes Midland Road (NC–2).

At 1.7 miles you'll pass Mid-Pines Plantation, a well-known golf resort and conference center. Then you'll pass several golf resorts on your right, surrounded by attractive residential areas. Longleaf pines line the roadsides and the medians, reinforcing the identity of the Sandhills.

Golf was first introduced in the Sandhills area around the turn of the century. This region already had several noted resorts where people came from the North to take the waters and improve their health. The introduction of golf fairly well cinched

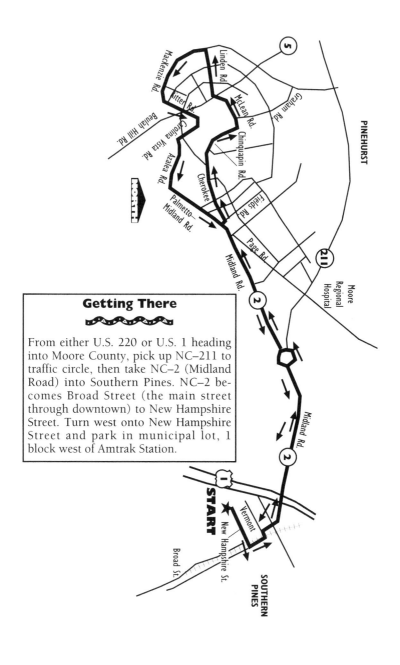

PINEHURST

Mackenzie Rd.

Linden Rd.

McLean Rd.

Graham Rd.

5

Ritter Rd.

Beulah Hill Rd.

Carolina Vista Rd.

Chinquapin Rd.

Azalea Rd.

Cherokee

Fields Rd.

Palmetto-
Midland Rd.

Page Rd.

Midland Rd.

211

2

Moore
Regional
Hospital

Getting There

From either U.S. 220 or U.S. 1 heading into Moore County, pick up NC–211 to traffic circle, then take NC–2 (Midland Road) into Southern Pines. NC–2 becomes Broad Street (the main street through downtown) to New Hampshire Street. Turn west onto New Hampshire Street and park in municipal lot, 1 block west of Amtrak Station.

Midland Rd.

2

1

START

Vermont

New Hampshire St.

Broad St.

SOUTHERN
PINES

NORTH

**DIREC-
TIONS
at a glance**

0.0 From intersection of Broad and New Hampshire Streets, turn left onto Broad Street.

0.2 Turn left onto Vermont Avenue, cross rail road tracks, and then turn right onto Northeast Broad Street (street becomes two-way at this point).

1.2 Cross under U.S. 1.

5.1 At traffic circle take Midland Road (NC–2), following signs to Pinehurst Village District.

6.0 Turn right onto Fields Road, then left onto Cherokee Avenue.

6.3 Turn right onto Chinquapin Road and follow through village shopping area.

7.0 Turn left onto Graham Road, then right onto McLean Road.

7.2 Cross Beulah Hill Road (NC–5) and bear left onto Linden Road.

7.7 Turn left onto MacKenzie Road.

8.1 Turn left onto Ritter Road. Cross Beulah Hill Road (NC–5).

8.3 Turn left into Pinehurst Hotel, circle through hotel drive and entrance, and then continue straight on Carolina Vista Road.

8.7 Turn left onto Azalea Road (NC–2), then make a 90-degree left turn onto Palmetto–Midland Road (NC–2).

10.0 At traffic circle, take Midland Road (NC–2) back toward Southern Pines.

15.6 Cross under U.S. 1.

16.8 Turn right onto New Hampshire Street and return to parking lot.

the area's draw as a resort location and has helped the area become known as the "golf capital of the world." More than thirty-five championship golf courses are located in the vicinity of Pinehurst.

At 5.1 miles you'll come to a large traffic circle—-or roundabout, as the British say—where you want to stay on Midland Road. Follow the signs to the Pinehurst Village District. The World Golf Hall of Fame, located off Midland Road (NC–2) in Pinehurst, not only pays tribute to famous golfers, but also celebrates the game of golf. On display in the museum section are golfing artifacts and memorabilia dating as far back as 1690.

The Pinehurst Village District has been carefully and intentionally preserved to show off the New England–style parks and roadways, which were laid out by Frederick Law Olmsted, the architect who designed New York's Central Park and Asheville's Biltmore Gardens. The town's streets are lined with handsome Georgian colonial homes and estates.

According to local lore, since Pinehurst was founded after Southern Pines and Southern Pines was laid out in a strict grid system, the designers of Pinehurst were instructed to do anything but a grid. The resulting curving maze of streets can be a challenge, even with a good map. But the route we've selected will show you a good cross section of the town without leaving you stranded.

One of the central showpieces of the town is the historic Pinehurst Hotel. As you cycle up the circular drive, you'll revel in the broad porches with awnings from another era stocked with plenty of old-fashioned rockers and ceiling fans, all overlooking beautiful gardens. You can see why people have been drawn to this resort for over one hundred years. Be sure to allow some time to stroll the neat sidewalks in the village area before heading back to Southern Pines via Midland Road.

Historic Tour of Southern Pines

Number of miles:	9.8
Approximate pedaling time:	1½ hours
Terrain:	Rolling
Traffic:	Light to moderate
Things to see:	Campbell House, Weymouth Center for the Arts and Humanities, Weymouth Woods Sandhills Nature Preserve, lovely large homes on wooded lots, quaint downtown area of Southern Pines with railroad tracks and huge magnolia trees
Food:	Along Broad Street in Southern Pines

Southern Pines has a very interesting history. It began as a health resort, which was developed by John Patrick in 1883. He named the streets after the New England states to get northerners to move south. Since Southern Pines is situated halfway between New York and Florida along the major north-south rail line, it was the ideal location for stopovers for northerners traveling to Florida for the winter or vice versa. As a result, about half a dozen large resort hotels were built in the town, and people started building their own English-style cottages around the hotels. They would spend November through January in Southern Pines, holding fox hunts and big parties until they moved on to Florida or New York.

The mild climate and sandy terrain with no rocks made the area ideal for horses—good footing—and for golf—no puddles on the golf courses. The two sports continue to be popular here today.

As you start the tour and go right on Vermont Avenue, you'll see some of the early Southern Pines houses that were small boardinghouses near the train station. Some were also tourist houses for people of less affluent means who were traveling through the area.

You'll cross North Ridge Street, which was the outer boundary on the original Southern Pines grid, and pass into the grounds of the Weymouth Center for the Arts and Humanities. James Boyd, grandson of the original owner, and his wife, Katharine, had the remaining portion of the original home redesigned about 1920 and used Weymouth for extensive entertaining for their literary and artistic friends. In honor of the Boyds, the estate now houses the Center for Arts and Humanities, including the North Carolina Literary Hall of Fame.

Across Connecticut Avenue is the other portion of James Boyd's original house, which his grandson Jack moved and later sold to the Campbells. It is now home to the Moore County Arts Council. On the right is the Train House, where Boyd's model trains are kept. As you travel out of town on Connecticut Avenue, you'll see several English Tudor houses that were originally built around the Highland Hotel. On your left is the beginning of Moore County's horse country.

The area along Highland Road is considered by some to be the prettiest block in Southern Pines. Some of these big houses are occupied only from October through May. The rest of the year the owners spend in Boston or other northern cities. As you turn right on Connecticut again you'll pass Duncraig Manor, which belongs to members of the Quaker Oats family. All the roads to the left are dirt for the benefit of the horses.

At 2.4 miles you'll see the beginning of the Weymouth Woods Nature Preserve, which contains the largest longleaf pine tree in North Carolina. Horse-riding trails interlace the area. At 4.8 miles you turn right onto Fort Bragg Road, so named because it skirts the perimeter of the military installation. Turn into Weymouth Woods at 6.5 miles and check out the Visitors Center, which has exhibits about how the pine forests were used

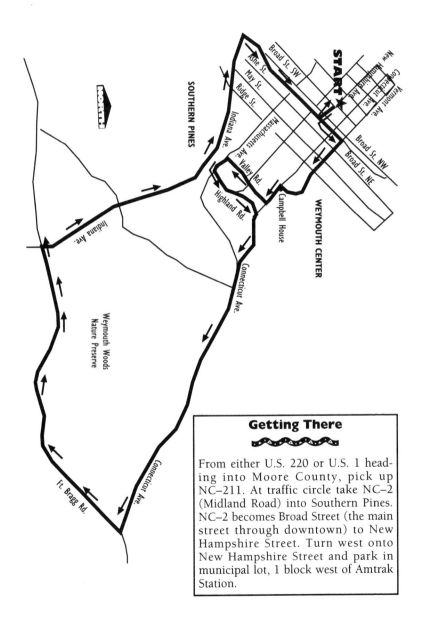

NORTH

START ★

Broad St. SW

Ashe St.

May St.

Ridge St.

Indiana Ave.

Massachusetts Ave.

Valley Rd.

Highland Rd.

Campbell House

SOUTHERN PINES

New Hampshire Ave.

Connecticut Ave.

Vermont Ave.

Broad St. NW

Broad St. NE

WEYMOUTH CENTER

Indiana Ave.

Weymouth Woods Nature Preserve

Connecticut Ave.

Connecticut Ave.

Ft. Bragg Rd.

Getting There

From either U.S. 220 or U.S. 1 heading into Moore County, pick up NC–211. At traffic circle take NC–2 (Midland Road) into Southern Pines. NC–2 becomes Broad Street (the main street through downtown) to New Hampshire Street. Turn west onto New Hampshire Street and park in municipal lot, 1 block west of Amtrak Station.

0.0 At intersection of Broad Street and New Hampshire Avenue, cross the railroad tracks and turn left onto Northeast Broad Street.

0.2 Turn right onto Vermont Avenue.

0.5 Cross North Ridge Street into Weymouth Center and bear right toward James Boyd House. Take exit from Weymouth Center and turn right onto Connecticut Avenue.

0.6 Turn left into Campbell House, turn around and come back out at Connecticut Avenue.

0.8 Turn right onto Connecticut Avenue.

1.0 Turn right on North Valley Road.

1.4 Turn left onto Massachusetts Avenue.

1.5 Turn left onto Highland Road.

1.9 Turn right onto Connecticut Avenue.

2.4 Beginning of nature preserve.

4.8 Turn right onto Fort Bragg Road.

6.5 Turn right into Weymouth Woods Nature Preserve. Turn around and return to Fort Bragg Road.

6.9 Turn right onto Fort Bragg Road.

7.4 Turn right onto Indiana Avenue.

9.4 Turn right onto Southeast Broad Street.

9.8 Turn left onto New Hampshire Avenue.

to produce turpentine and other naval stores.

As you come back into Southern Pines on Southeast Broad Street, you'll pass the Princess Movie Theater on the right—now an antiques store—which was the first talking-movie theater in North Carolina. Enjoy the gorgeous magnolia trees that line the railroad tracks through the middle of town. You can see how the railroad was literally the lifeblood of this town for so many years and still carries passengers to and from the Amtrak station on Broad Street.

Horse Country Loop:
Moore County

Number of miles:	22.5
Approximate pedaling time:	2 hours
Terrain:	Rolling, with some good ups and downs
Traffic:	Light to moderate
Things to see:	Campbell House, horse farms, houses with stables underneath, Equine Hospital and Equine Center
Food:	In Southern Pines, convenience store after you cross U.S. 1 in Lakeview; country stores in Lakeview and Niagara

It won't take you long to see why this tour is called Horse Country Loop. Thoroughbreds will lazily glance at you as you pass their lush pastures and luxurious accommodations. There are also caution signs for horseback riders and for horses and carriages all along the route. In fact, this part of Moore County is so engrossed in horses that deeds for the farms in this area are especially drawn up to allow horseback riders to cross the property of others.

The horse people in the area can be divided into three interest groups: the hunter-jumpers, the fox hunters, and the carriage drivers. The hunter-jumpers participate in three-day events for dressage, cross-country, and stadium. Carriage drivers have four special horse shows in the fall and four more in the spring. Some old photographs of Southern Pines show the fox hunters coming right through the center of town on Broad Street. Horses are so important to these people that many build their own living quarters over the stables that house their horses. Watch for these along the route—many are situated away from the road, so you have to really look.

Pappy and Ginny Moss were original horse lovers in the area who established the Moss Foundation to preserve open land for horseback riding. In many places you'll see sandy, dirt roads crossing the paved ones to allow gentler surfaces for the horses' hooves.

As you head right on Youngs Road (SR 2026), you'll pass through a residential area with lots of longleaf pines. But soon you'll see the miles of horse fences and farms with names like Economy Farm, Greedy Mother Farm, Land's End, and Sweet and Sourwood Farm. A tobacco field here and there keeps the horse pastures from totally dominating the region.

The rolling hills along Lakebay Road (SR 2023) frame even more horse farms (after about 4.5 miles). Look along here for the houses with the stables underneath. After you cross U.S. 1 and the railroad tracks in Lakeview (convenience store at the intersection), you'll see Crystal Lake on the left. After you turn right on Airport Road (SR 1843), there's a sharp turn after the next 0.1 mile. Niagara-Carthage Road (SR 1802) at 16.3 miles is wider, with slight paved shoulders. More horse farms are situated along the left side of this road.

On Valley View Road (SR 1857) after 19.3 miles, you'll pass the Equine Hospital and Equine Center with lots of practice fields for riding and jumping. This road merges into North May Street (SR 2080) after 1.1 miles.

When you return to the Campbell House, take some time to visit. Originally a private home, Campbell House was given to the Town of Southern Pines by Major and Mrs. W. D. Campbell in 1966 to serve "the cultural and social enrichment of the inhabitants of the community." The house's large room—called the Board Room or Permanent Gallery—was part of the Boyd home built in 1903 on the site of the present Weymouth Center. In the 1920s, grandsons of the original Boyd moved this part of the house to its current site on Connecticut Avenue, where it became Jack Boyd's home.

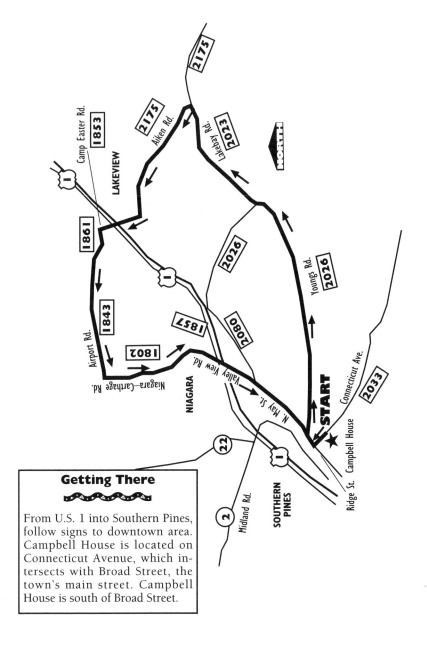

Getting There

From U.S. 1 into Southern Pines, follow signs to downtown area. Campbell House is located on Connecticut Avenue, which intersects with Broad Street, the town's main street. Campbell House is south of Broad Street.

DIREC-TIONS at a glance

0.0 From Campbell House on Connecticut Avenue in Southern Pines, turn left onto Connecticut Avenue.

0.1 Turn right onto Ridge Street.

4.1 Turn right onto Youngs Road (SR 2026).

9.4 Turn right onto Lakebay Road (SR 2023).

12.4 Turn left onto Aiken Road (SR 2175) to Lakeview; cross U.S. 1 and continue on Camp Easter Road (SR 1853).

12.8 Turn left on SR 1861.

13.1 Turn right onto Airport Road (SR 1843).

16.3 Turn left onto Niagara-Carthage Road (SR 1802) and follow into Niagara.

19.2 Arrive Niagara; continue on Niagara–Carthage Road (SR 1802).

19.3 Turn right onto Valley View Road (SR 1857).

20.3 Valley View Road (SR 1857) merges with North May Street (SR 2080).

22.3 Turn left onto Connecticut Avenue.

22.5 Turn right into Campbell House.

The house grew with new additions. Then in 1946 Major Campbell bought the property and made extensive changes. The original frame house was faced with valuable old ballast brick from Charleston, S.C. The house now serves as an exhibition center for local artists and a meeting place for about twenty-five organizations.

Ellerbe to Hamlet:
Richmond County

Number of miles:	33.7
Approximate pedaling time:	3½ hours
Terrain:	Rolling, with a few short, moderate hills
Traffic:	Light except in towns
Things to see:	Rankin Museum of American Heritage, National Railroad Museum, Historic Rockingham, Historic Hamlet, stately homes, quaint towns
Food:	In towns of Ellerbe, Rockingham, and Hamlet

The Rankin Museum, our starting point for this route, includes a diverse collection of cultural artifacts and natural history items from South America to the Arctic and from Africa to Alaska. Here you can see an arctic polar bear, a Central American jaguar, fossils from the Paleozoic era, and an eclectic collection of rocks, minerals, and gems—many from Richmond County. Artifacts of North Carolina pottery, nineteenth-century tools, and beadwork from the Plains Indians of North America are some of the other interesting exhibits in this most varied collection. Try to spend some time here, although museum hours are somewhat limited—10:00 A.M. to 4:00 P.M. Tuesday through Friday and 2:00 to 5:00 P.M. Saturday and Sunday. Admission is $2.00 for adults and $1.00 for students.

From Ellerbe, its Main Street lined with antiques shops, we head across country on smooth pavement to enjoy the forests and rolling terrain. Pine forests, so typical of the Sandhills region, abound but are interspersed by lush pastures where horses graze.

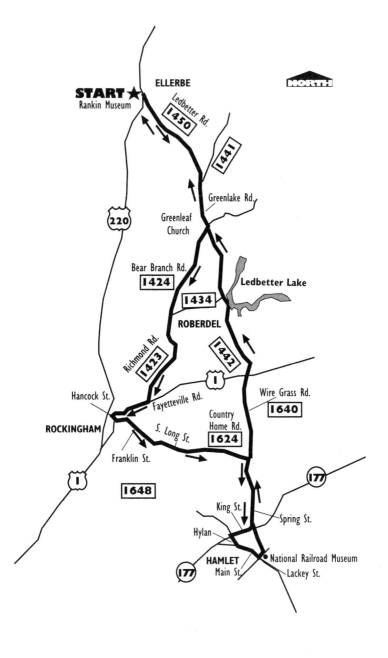

DIREC-TIONS at a glance

0.0 From intersection of Church and Main Streets, turn right onto Main Street. *Note:* Some roads on route may not have state road number signs.

0.3 Turn left onto Ledbetter Road (SR 1450), also Bike Route 23. Ledbetter Road name changes to Greenlake Road but remains SR 1450.

3.3 Bear right when SR 1450 merges with SR 1441; name remains Greenlake Road.

4.3 Turn right onto Bear Branch Road (SR 1424), the name of which changes to Roberdel Road after you pass Roberdel community.

8.4 Turn right onto Richmond Road (SR 1423).

10.1 Turn right onto Fayetteville Road (U.S. 1) toward Rock ingham.

10.9 Bear right on U.S. 1 but stay in left lane on one-way street.

11.2 Turn left onto Hancock Street (U.S. 1).

11.3 Turn left onto Franklin Street (U.S. 1 North).

11.5 Bear right onto Rockingham Road (SR 1648).

12.8 Turn left onto South Long Street at light (hospital is on left), then make an immediate right turn onto County Home Road (SR 1624).

15.8 Turn right onto Wire Grass Road (SR 1640) going into Hamlet.

17.7 Turn left onto Spring Street.

17.8 Turn right onto King Street (NC–177 South).

Getting There

From U.S. 220, drive into town of Ellerbe, where U.S. 220 becomes Main Street, and turn west onto Church Street (there's a large Citgo station on the corner—street signs are not highly visible). Rankin Museum of American Heritage is on left in second block. Parking is available in front of the museum.

18.4 Turn left onto Hylan Avenue.

18.5 Turn left onto Main Street in Hamlet.

19.0 Turn left onto Lackey Street.

19.1 Turn right into Old Seaboard Railroad Station on exit, go right on Lackey Street. (Name changes to Raleigh Street across the tracks.).

19.5 Turn left onto Spring Street (one-way street).

20.2 Turn right onto Wire Grass Road (SR 1640). Continue straight past the intersection with County Home Road (SR 1624).

24.4 Cross U.S. 1.

24.7 Turn left onto Ledbetter Road (SR 1442).

26.6 Turn left onto Greenlake Road (SR 1441).

29.1 At intersection by Greenleaf Church, road number changes from SR 1441 to SR 1450. Greenlake Road name changes back to Ledbetter Road in Ellerbe.

33.4 Turn right onto Main Street (U.S. 220) in Ellerbe.

33.7 Turn left onto Church Street to return to Rankin Museum.

At 4.3 miles, where you turn right on Bear Branch Road (SR 1424), you'll see the pretty white building of Greenleaf Church, an example of the historic churches in the county. The churches, or meetinghouses, served as a stabilizing force for law and order in the early wilderness and had a profound influence on the lives of those hearty early settlers. After passing through scrub forests, you reach the small community of Roberdel, with its cluster of neat frame houses. After a sharp bend in the road and a short climb, Bear Branch Road's name changes to Roberdel Road.

As you enter Rockingham, Fayetteville Road (U.S. 1) takes you past the Historic District, with its many restored homes from the late nineteenth and early twentieth centuries. In the downtown area you'll circle the Richmond County Courthouse (built in 1922) and the U.S. Federal Building (1935), both of which are on the National Register of Historic Places. Rockingham serves as the county seat of Richmond County.

As you pedal toward Hamlet on County Home Road (SR 1624), you'll see a wide variety of homes. Note the sandy soil of the area. The sand remains from a large dune system that in prehistoric times was the edge of the sea, which came this far inland. Wire Grass Road (SR 1640), named for the popular roadside plant in this area, has ups and downs as it leads into Hamlet. The large stately homes along Main Street point to the Historic District, which lies off to the right. Be careful of the road edges in Hamlet because even where there are curbs, the repaving has left a 2-to-3-inch drop-off in many places.

Hamlet is home to the National Railroad Museum, housed in the old Seaboard Railroad Station off Lackey Street. The entrance to the museum is on the track side of the buildings. The distinctive architecture of this building alone makes it worth a stop. As you leave the station, you'll go right on Lackey Street, the name of which changes to Raleigh Street when you cross the tracks. At the intersection of Raleigh Street and Hamlet Avenue, be especially careful because this one block covers a busy section of U.S. 74 through Hamlet. Stay in the left lane so you're in the proper position to turn left onto Spring Street at the next light.

Just after you turn left onto Ledbetter Road (SR 1442), look on your right for the dam and waterfall for Ledbetter Lake. This road takes you back to Ellerbe, the center point for many fruit and vegetable farms in the area. In the summer many produce stands operate in the vicinity, especially when local peaches are ripe.

St. Andrews in Scotland County

Number of miles:	22.0
Approximate pedaling time:	2 hours
Terrain:	Relatively flat, with a few small hills
Traffic:	Very light except along Main Street
Things to see:	St. Andrews Presbyterian College campus, cypress stands in area lakes, historic churches, lovely old farmhouses, soybean fields
Food:	Along U.S. 15/401 Business in Laurinburg and in Laurel Hill

This tour begins on the lovely campus of St. Andrews Presbyterian College in Laurinburg. With a relatively young campus built in the late 1950s, St. Andrews presents a contemporary and well-thought-out campus with a unified architectural style. The new college opened its doors in 1961, consolidating the programs of Flora McDonald College (for women) and Presbyterian Junior College (for men). Take some time to walk around the campus and cross the large lake, the college's centerpiece.

As you can imagine, Scotland County takes its name from the homeland of many of the settlers in this area, who had names like McNair and McLaurin. Since many of these folks were brought up in the Calvinist tradition, there are many Presbyterian churches in the area. These congregations banded together with business leaders in the community to raise enough money to have the new college built here. In subsequent years new manufacturing plants and other businesses have found Scotland County an attractive place to locate.

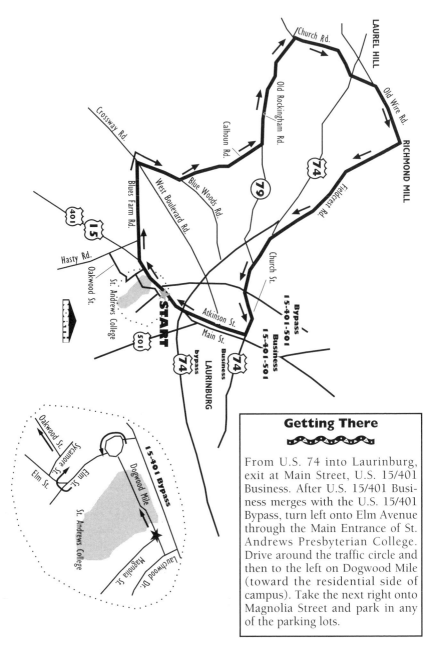

Getting There

From U.S. 74 into Laurinburg, exit at Main Street, U.S. 15/401 Business. After U.S. 15/401 Business merges with the U.S. 15/401 Bypass, turn left onto Elm Avenue through the Main Entrance of St. Andrews Presbyterian College. Drive around the traffic circle and then to the left on Dogwood Mile (toward the residential side of campus). Take the next right onto Magnolia Street and park in any of the parking lots.

DIREC-TIONS at a glance

0.0 From intersection of Magnolia Street and Dogwood Mile, turn left onto Dogwood Mile.

0.6 At traffic circle, bear left and then travel three-quarters of the way around.

0.9 Turn right onto Elm Avenue toward Scotia Village.

1.4 Turn right onto Sycamore Street (SR 1632).

2.0 Turn left onto Oakwood (SR 1608).

2.4 Turn right onto Hasty Road (SR 1615).

2.6 Cross U.S. 15/401.

3.0 Turn left onto Blues Farm Road (SR 1117).

5.2 Turn right onto Crossway Road (SR 1008). (Sign says X-way Road.)

5.3 Turn left onto Blue Woods Road (SR 1116).

6.0 Turn left onto Calhoun Road (SR 1119).

7.8 Turn left onto NC–79 at Springfield Mills.

8.3 Turn right onto Old Rockingham Road (SR 1126).

10.0 Turn right onto St. Johns Church Rd. (SR 1148).

11.4 When you cross U.S. 74, St. Johns Church Road name changes to Morgan Street (SR 1001) in Laurel Hill.

12.0 Bear right onto Old Wire Road (SR 1319).

14.8 Turn right onto Fieldcrest Road.

18.0 Turn left onto U.S. 74 Business, which becomes West Church Street in Laurinburg.

20.0 Turn right onto Atkinson Street.

21.2 Turn right onto Main Street. (After you cross under U.S. 74 Bypass, prepare to turn left at second light.)

21.8 Turn left onto Lauchwood Drive, then immediately right onto Dogwood Mile on the St. Andrews campus.

22.0 Turn left onto Magnolia Street to parking lots.

As you leave the campus, you'll head toward Scotia Village, a large retirement community affiliated with the college. After crossing the busy McColl Road (U.S. 15/401), you'll head out into the country on Blues Farm Road (SR 1117) past pine forests and pleasant residential areas. The Lakeview development is built around a typical lake for the area, featuring stands of cypress trees and populated with ducks and swans. X-way Road (SR 1008) leads to the community of Crossway, the site of the old X-way Mill.

Calhoun Road (SR 1119) bisects large fields of soybeans and corn, then forests on either side. You pass through Livingston Quarters before arriving in the pleasant community of Laurel Hill. St. Johns Church Road (SR 1148) changes both name and number after you cross U.S. 74 to Morgan Street (SR 1001). At 12.0 miles bear right on Old Wire Road (SR 1319) and watch for an old, but active mill wheel on the left at 12.7 miles. Tobacco fields, too, are around, but not as plentiful as in other parts of the state.

Richmond Mills, with its requisite millpond, was the site of a cannon factory during the Civil War. Contemporary textile industries are situated along Fieldcrest Road (SR 1303)—a large plant for Champion sportswear and another for Mohawk Yarns. U.S. 74 Business has only light-to-moderate traffic because most through traffic takes the bypass. As you enter Laurinburg, the road turns into West Church Street, edged with stately homes and two large churches, one of which is Presbyterian.

Atkinson Street, which parallels tree-lined Main Street, has magnificent trees of its own and less traffic. Atkinson ends at a more southern point on Main Street, where you face 0.6 mile of fairly heavy traffic because so many fast-food restaurants are along this part of the highway. Numerous traffic lights slow the traffic and allow cyclists to negotiate their way into the turn lane to return to the St. Andrews campus via the second entrance on the residential side of the lake.

Biking Bald Head:
Bald Head Island

Number of miles:	About 8
Approximate pedaling time:	1¼ hours
Terrain:	Flat
Traffic:	Only golf carts and other bicycles
Things to see:	Maritime forests, nature trails, gazebo at the beach, beautiful beaches, Bald Head Lighthouse, beautiful marina
Food:	Several restaurants in the marina area

Bald Head Island, North Carolina's southernmost cape island, possesses one of the East Coast's most stunning examples of maritime forest, composed of stately live oak trees centuries old, dogwoods, yaupon, wax myrtle, cedar, and palmetto trees. The most prominent landmark on the island is Old Baldy, the 1817 Bald Head Lighthouse, the second of three lighthouses built on the island and the only one remaining. The lighthouse was decommissioned in 1903 when the Cape Fear Light was constructed on the easternmost point of the island. Thanks to restoration efforts by the Old Baldy Foundation and generous contributions from supporters, the lighthouse is open to visitors who wish to climb its 108 steps for a spectacular panoramic view.

The 12,000-acre island includes Cape Fear and Frying Pan Shoals, an underwater labyrinth of sandbars that stretches for 20 miles into the Atlantic Ocean. These sandbars, which vary in depth from 3 to 15 feet, make navigating the cape a bit tricky. Cape Fear, Cape Hatteras, and Cape Lookout are collectively known as the Graveyard of the Atlantic because of the numerous shipwrecks that have occurred along this stretch of coast. Fortunately the sandbars also create excellent fishing conditions that

attract tourists from all over. Because of the island's unique geographic location, the sun both rises and sets over the Atlantic Ocean.

Bald Head Island, to quote the official vacation planner, "is different from other coastal resort communities because it's not slick, honky-tonk, or highbrow. There are no water slides, traffic lights, or tourist traps." The island got its name from the river pilots who were so eager to offer their services to ships approaching the entrance to the Cape Fear River that they wore the top of the headland bare by taking up watch there. This "bald" headland contrasted with the marine forest behind it, making it a reference point for navigators.

Through the years the island has been a breeding ground for wild boar, a safe haven for pirates, and a nesting ground for loggerhead turtles. Protection of the turtles continues to this day, and the Bald Head Island Conservancy Headquarters near the Cape Fear end of the island has educational exhibits on the turtles as well as fund-raising items for sale.

The gazebo on East Beach offers a shady resting spot and access to the pristine and unpolluted beach. The Maritime Forest Preserve in the south-central part of the island contains the Kent Mitchell Nature Trail. It affords a twenty-minute walk through the forest and along the salt marsh and tidal creek, with various plant species labeled along the way. In the summer months the Bald Head Island Conservancy conducts turtle walks at night and alligator and bird walks in the morning.

One of the most interesting aspects of Bald Head is its 10,000 acres of protected salt marshes and tidal creeks. The Bald Head Island Conservancy oversees the conservation of this vital area, ensuring the survival of the endangered loggerhead turtle through its Sea Turtle Nest Protection Project. The island naturalist supervises nest monitoring and hatchling emergence activities for research and education.

Bald Head offers an unusual, scenic, and restful retreat in a unique environment. Although you may not cover a lot of miles on your bike, you'll enjoy the discoveries you make along the way.

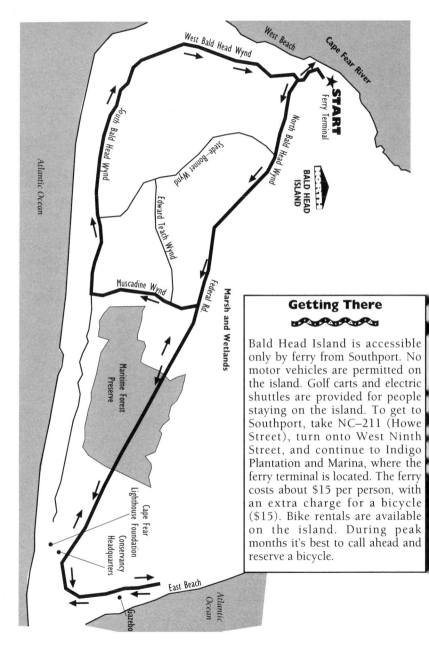

West Bald Head Wynd

West Beach

Cape Fear River

★ START
Ferry Terminal

BALD HEAD ISLAND

South Bald Head Wynd

North Bald Head Wynd

Stede-Bonnet Wynd

Edward Teach Wynd

Atlantic Ocean

Muscadine Wynd

Federal Rd.

Marsh and Wetlands

Maritime Forest Preserve

Cape Fear Lighthouse Foundation

Conservancy Headquarters

East Beach

Atlantic Ocean

Gazebo

Getting There

Bald Head Island is accessible only by ferry from Southport. No motor vehicles are permitted on the island. Golf carts and electric shuttles are provided for people staying on the island. To get to Southport, take NC–211 (Howe Street), turn onto West Ninth Street, and continue to Indigo Plantation and Marina, where the ferry terminal is located. The ferry costs about $15 per person, with an extra charge for a bicycle ($15). Bike rentals are available on the island. During peak months it's best to call ahead and reserve a bicycle.

DIREC-TIONS at a glance

Start at the ferry landing on the island, heading toward the East Beach gazebo at the other end of the island. (The distances are so short and the island so small that mileage is not given here.)

- Turn left out of parking lot for ferry landing.
- Turn right onto Keelson Row, and then almost immediately turn left onto North Bald Head Wynd.
- Continue straight on North Bald Head Wynd past turnoff for Stede-Bonnet Wynd.
- North Bald Head Wynd becomes Federal Road.
- Continue straight on Federal Road, passing turnoff for Muscadine Wynd, to the gazebo at East Beach (public beach access at this point).
- Turn around and begin to retrace route on Federal Road.
- Turn left onto Muscadine Wynd.
- Continue straight on Muscadine Wynd past turnoff for Edward Teach Wynd.
- Turn right onto South Bald Head Wynd.
- Continue straight on South Bald Head Wynd past turnoff for Stede-Bonnet Wynd.
- South Bald Head Wynd turns into West Bald Head Wynd where the road curves.
- Continue on West Bald Head Wynd bearing left on Keelson Row just past North Bald Head Wynd.
- Turn left into parking lot for ferry landing.

Southport to Orton Plantation

Number of miles:	31.9
Approximate pedaling time:	2½ hours
Terrain:	Flat
Traffic:	Light to moderate
Things to see:	Historic Southport, Orton Plantation Gardens, Brunswick Town Historic Site, historic Wilmington, Battleship North Carolina (nearby)
Food:	Restaurants in Southport, snacks at Orton Plantation

You'll step back in history on this tour from historic Southport at the mouth of the Cape Fear River to majestic Orton Plantation and Brunswick Town. Southport is situated halfway between New York and Miami on the Intracoastal Waterway, making it the perfect stopping point for yachts and other seacraft. Located on a bluff at the mouth of the river, Southport was the ideal location for Fort Johnson, built in 1764, the state's first fort. After being destroyed by fire in 1775, the fort was rebuilt and today houses the Commanding Officer of the Sunny Point Military Ocean Terminal. While you're in Southport you may want to visit the Southport Maritime Museum, whose exhibits preserve the rich maritime history of the area. Admission is $2.00 for adults, aged 16 and older.

As you exit Southport on North Howe Street, you'll appreciate the wide lanes and the Bike Route 3 signs marking the way. After you turn onto NC–87 North at about 1.8 miles, you'll see on your right the sign for the Visitors Center at the Carolina

Power & Light (CP&L) Brunswick Nuclear Power Plant. The center presents more than thirty energy-related exhibits on the production of electricity, safety, alternative energy sources, and energy conservation. Admission is free.

Once you're on NC–133 after NC–87 has turned north, you'll enjoy the coolness of the forests on either side. The road is paved but a little rough in this section. You'll enter the grounds of Orton Plantation on a hard-packed sandy road whose length is lined with trees, just like something out of *Gone with the Wind*. Gray-blue Spanish moss drapes gracefully from the huge live oak trees guarding the entrance. Initially a rice plantation, Orton was constructed in 1715. Orton House, a central feature of the plantation, represents a nearly perfect example of antebellum, Greek Revival architecture in the South—reminiscent of the fictional Tara. The home is still a private residence, not open for visitors, but you can enjoy its beauty as you stroll through the gardens.

Although the gardens have something to offer any time of year, spring is one of the most glorious times when azaleas, dogwoods, camellias, roses, and flowering fruit trees are at their peak. May and June bring blooms to daylilies, oleander, rhododendrons, gardenias, magnolias, and irises. Crape myrtles and summer annuals add color to the garden during July and August. On warm days alligators sun themselves on the banks of the marshy areas.

From Orton Plantation you'll ride a short distance to Brunswick Town Historic Site along the Scenic Byway. The excavated ruins of the colonial port town are open to visitors who wish to learn more about life during colonial times in coastal North Carolina. One of the leading seaports in colonial North Carolina, the town lost most of its residents when the Revolutionary War started; few of those who fled returned. During the Civil War Confederates built Fort Anderson near the site of the old town. Soldiers there held out for thirty days after Fort Fisher fell but finally abandoned the fort after a three-day siege. The visitors center at the site offers a slide show and exhibits about the area.

When you return to Southport, you may want to visit Water-

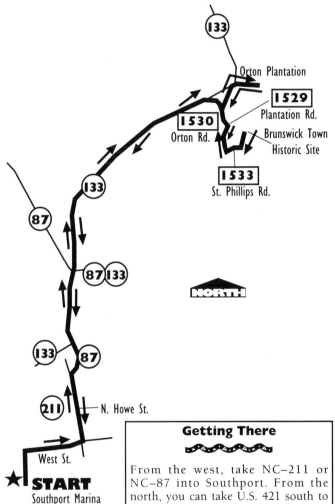

133

Orton Plantation

1529
Plantation Rd.

1530
Orton Rd.

Brunswick Town
Historic Site

1533
St. Phillips Rd.

133

87

87 133

NORTH

133 87

211 — N. Howe St.

West St.

★ **START**
Southport Marina

Getting There

From the west, take NC–211 or
NC–87 into Southport. From the
north, you can take U.S. 421 south to
Fort Fisher, then take the ferry to
Southport. The Southport Marina and
public parking area are located at the
end of West Street, which intersects
with North Howe Street (NC–87).

DIREC-TIONS at a glance

0.0 From Southport Marina public parking lot, head out toward street.

0.1 Turn right at stop sign onto West Street.

0.5 Turn left onto North Howe Street (Bike Route 3).

1.8 Turn right onto NC–87 North.

3.1 NC–133 joins NC–87; continue straight.

5.1 Continue straight on NC–133 (NC–87 goes off to left).

12.6 Turn right onto Orton Road (SR 1530).

12.9 Turn left onto Plantation Road (SR 1529).

13.0 Turn right into Orton Plantation.

13.7 Go in entrance to gardens or take circular drive to exit.

14.6 Turn left onto Plantation Road (SR 1529) toward Brunswick Town.

16.2 Turn left onto St. Phillips Road (SR 1533).

16.6 Entrance to Brunswick Town; turn right toward visitors center.

16.8 Arrive at visitors center. Turn around and retrace route to Brunswick Town entrance.

17.4 Turn right onto Plantation Road (SR 1529).

19.0 Turn left onto Orton Road (SR 1530).

19.3 Turn left onto NC–133.

26.8 Stay straight on NC–133; NC–133 joins NC–87.

28.8 Stay straight on NC–87 (NC–133 goes off to right).

30.1 NC–87 ends. Turn left onto NC–211, which turns into Howe Street in Southport.

31.4 Turn right onto West Street.

31.9 Turn left into parking lot at marina.

front Park, the town's most popular park. That's because from the park, you have the perfect vantage point for watching transoceanic vessels from around the world as they glide up the Cape Fear River to the state ports in Wilmington.

Swansboro Bicentennial Trail

Number of miles:	26.8
Approximate pedaling time:	2½ hours
Terrain:	Mostly flat
Traffic:	Heavy along NC–24 and NC–58, otherwise light to moderate, depending on time of day
Things to see:	Cedar Point Recreation Area, White Oak Chapel, Hadnot's Creek Primitive Baptist Church, Croatan National Forest, Bear Island, and Hammock's Beach State Park are nearby
Food:	Restaurants in Swansboro, convenience stores and service stations in small communities along route

Named for Samuel Swann, the town was incorporated as Swannsborough in 1783. The port area from the White Oak River to Bogue Inlet was established in 1786. Like many seacoast towns, its primary industries were shipbuilding, trade, and commercial fishing. During times of war the manufacturing of salt from seawater became important, and Swansboro played a significant role.

Ardent patriots established a warehouse there during the Revolutionary War to supply the Continental Army. During the War of 1812, Captain Otway Burns—North Carolina's most famous privateer—sailed from Swansboro. During the Civil War, Union forces captured the town three times.

Now a retirement center and tourist area, Swansboro has taken on a new role and one hospitable to cyclists. As you begin the tour, be careful on the short stretch of NC–24 you must travel to before heading north. NC–58 is also very busy, but the route snakes back and forth across that state highway so you can avoid a lot of the heavy traffic.

The Cedar Point Recreation Area, off to the left after you turn onto Old NC–58 (SR 1113), provides hiking trails, picnicking, drinking water, and overnight camping facilities. Cypress boardwalks help visitors cross the tidal marshes to explore the unusual habitat of the Croatan National Forest.

Two miles north of the junction of NC–24 and NC–58 is the Crystal Coast Amphitheater, where the outdoor drama *Worthy Is the Lamb* is produced during the summer months. The three-hour musical drama tells the life of Jesus using boats, horses, camels, chariots, and a soundtrack recorded in England by Shakespearean actors, choral groups, and a symphony orchestra.

On Whitehorse Fork Road (SR 1111) is White Oak Chapel, which was established in 1901 as a Unitarian church, part of a field of four Unitarian churches established as a mission with an impressive social and educational program, headquartered in Swansboro. Today the chapel building is used as the Pelletier Community Building.

Just before you cross Hadnot Creek on Old Church Road (SR 1104), you'll see Hadnot's Creek Primitive Baptist Church, whose congregation was established at least as early as 1790. The existing church was built about 1840 and is the only remaining landmark of Pelletier's Mills community with its water-powered gristmill.

This part of the route in Carteret County skirts the Croatan National Forest, which covers 155,000 acres of coastal land. The abundant wildlife here includes several rare or endangered species, such as the bald eagle, the peregrine falcon, and the red-cockcaded woodpecker. Alligators inhabit the deep swamps and waterways, although they are generally retiring, preferring to sun themselves on logs and banks. The wet upland bogs are home to several unusual carnivorous plants, such as the Venus flytrap and the pitcher plant.

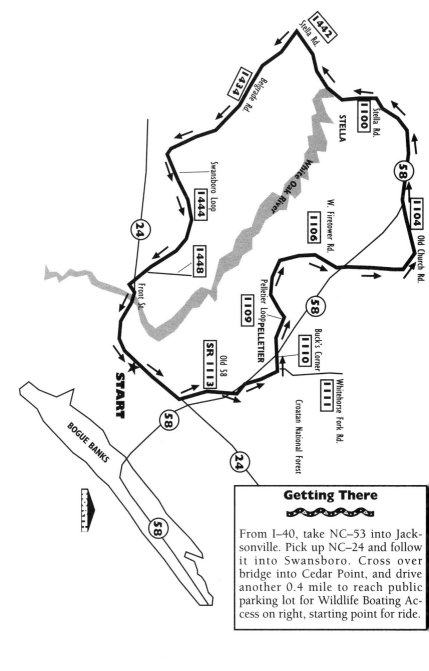

1442
Stella Rd.

1434
Belgrade Rd.

STELLA
1100
Stella Rd.

58

1104
Old Church Rd.

Swansboro Loop
1444

White Oak River

W. Firetower Rd.
1106

1448

58

Pelletier Loop PELLETIER
1109

Front St.

Buck's Corner
1110

Whitehorse Fork Rd.
1111

SR 1113
Old 58

START

58

Croatan National Forest

24

BOGUE BANKS

58

58

24

Getting There

From I–40, take NC–53 into Jacksonville. Pick up NC–24 and follow it into Swansboro. Cross over bridge into Cedar Point, and drive another 0.4 mile to reach public parking lot for Wildlife Boating Access on right, starting point for ride.

DIREC-TIONS at a glance

0.0	From public parking lot for Wildlife Boating Access, turn right onto NC–24.
2.3	Turn left onto Old NC–58 (SR 1113).
3.0	Turn right and then left onto NC–58.
4.2	Turn right onto Whitehorse Fork Road (SR 1111).
4.4	Sharp curve to left.
5.0	Turn left onto Buck's Corner (SR 1110).
5.4	Turn right onto NC–58.
5.5	Turn left onto Pelletier Loop (SR 1109).
6.3	Turn left onto West Firetower Road (SR 1106).
7.5	Turn right to stay on West Firetower Road (SR 1106).
9.2	Cross NC–58 onto Old Church Road (SR 1104).
12.7	Turn right onto NC–58.
14.1	Turn left onto Stella Road (SR 1100/1442).
16.0	Stay on Stella Road when state route number changes to 1442.
17.9	Turn left onto Belgrade in Swansboro (SR 1434).
21.9	Turn left onto Swansboro Loop (SR 1444).
25.2	Turn left onto Main Street. SR 1448 goes left to the White Oak River.
25.7	Continue straight across NC–24.
25.8	Turn left onto Front Street.
25.9	Turn right onto NC–24 across bridge.
26.8	Turn right into parking lot.

The quaint town itself offers picturesque views of the marina and harbor as well as interesting shops in which to browse. If you're so inclined, a passenger ferry will take you across the water to Bear Island, home to the 890 acres of Hammock's Beach State Park.

Bicycling through Beautiful Beaufort

Number of miles:	5.2
Approximate pedaling time:	¾ hour
Terrain:	Flat
Traffic:	Light except along Front Street
Things to see:	Beaufort waterfront, marinas, historic houses, interesting shops, North Carolina Maritime Museum
Food:	Restaurants and snack shops along Front Street

Settled in 1709, Beaufort (pronounced *BO-fort,* as opposed to the South Carolina pronunciation for the city with the same spelling, *BEW-firt*) is North Carolina's third oldest town. First surveyed in 1713, the town was well established before George Washington was even born. Named for Henry Somerset, Duke of Beaufort in England, the town was incorporated in 1723 and has been the county seat of Carteret County ever since.

Originally a fishing village and port of safety dating from the 1600s, Beaufort has been visited by patriots, privateers, and pirates. Today, its marinas and attractive waterfront area attract boaters and tourists from all over. Our tour crisscrosses the historic area and gives you the flavor of what makes Beaufort special.

The Historic District of Beaufort, listed on the National Register of Historic Places, includes more than one hundred historic homes, with plaques bearing their names and dates of construction. The Old Burying Ground, listed separately on the National Register, dates from the early 1700s and includes the remains of many whose lives would make interesting tales. The earliest leg-

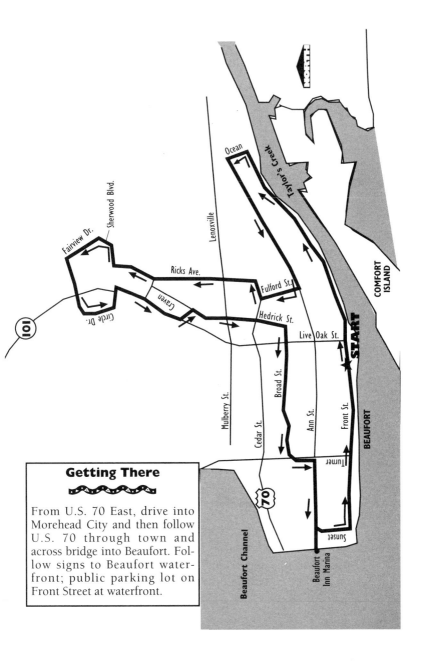

NORTH

Ocean

Taylor's Creek

Sherwood Blvd.

Fairview Dr.

Lenoxville

Ricks Ave.

Fulford St.

Craven

Circle Dr.

Hedrick St.

COMFORT ISLAND

101

Live Oak St.

START

Mulberry St.

Broad St.

Ann St.

Front St.

BEAUFORT

Cedar St.

Turner

70

Sunset

Beaufort Channel

Beaufort Inn Marina

Getting There

From U.S. 70 East, drive into Morehead City and then follow U.S. 70 through town and across bridge into Beaufort. Follow signs to Beaufort waterfront; public parking lot on Front Street at waterfront.

0.0 From waterfront public parking lot, turn right onto Front Street.
1.1 Turn left onto Ocean Street.
1.2 Turn left onto Ann Street.
1.7 Turn right onto Fulford Street.
1.9 Turn right onto Cedar/Third Street (street seems to have two names).
2.3 Turn right onto Ricks Avenue.
2.5 Turn right onto Sherwood Boulevard.
2.8 Turn left onto Fairview Drive and cross Live Oak Street onto Circle Drive.
3.2 Turn right onto Live Oak Street.
3.4 Turn left onto First Street.
3.5 Turn right onto Craven Avenue, crossing Lenoxville Street and bearing left onto Hedrick Street.
3.8 Turn right onto Broad Street.
4.3 Turn left onto Turner Street.
4.4 Turn right onto Ann Street.
4.7 Enter Beaufort Inn Marina and turn around.
4.8 Turn right into alley (no street sign).
4.9 Turn left onto Front Street.
5.2 Turn right into parking lot.

ible marker there dates from 1756. All the graves face east in the oldest portion so that the occupants would face the sun on Judgment Morn.

Take some time to wander the waterfront and explore the interesting shops, many of them with handcrafted items. One of the first sights you'll see along Front Street is the North Carolina Maritime Museum, which houses a collection of natural and maritime history exhibits, ship models, and outstanding shell collections. The museum also offers a variety of field trips, lectures, and programs for all ages. Admission is free.

The first part of the tour along Front Street takes you along the waterfront where you can look across Taylor's Creek to Carrot Island. Wild ponies live on the island and sometimes are visible as they graze on the various island grasses. After you turn on Ocean Street, you'll go 1 block before turning again on Ann Street, named for Queen Anne of England, who was on the throne when the town was founded. Many of the other streets are named for nobility of the time: Craven Street for the Earl of Craven; Turner Street for Robert Turner, who owned the land that was surveyed; and Orange Street for William, Prince of Orange, who became William III of England.

As you travel the route, look for the interesting architecture and historic plaques. Among the historic buildings you're likely to see are these: the R. Rustell House (c. 1732), with its tin roof and frame construction, used as an art gallery in spring and summer; the Joseph Bell House (c. 1767), former home of a well-to-do plantation owner, painted conch red with white shutters—a beautiful example of early Beaufort architecture; Samuel Leffer's Cottage (c. 1778), a schoolmaster's dwelling, a restored building with a typical early Beaufort roofline; Carteret County Courthouse of 1796, the oldest remaining public building in Carteret County, used as the meeting place for the Church of England before 1796 and authentically furnished for the period, including an original thirteen-star American flag; the Josiah Bell House (c. 1825), furnished in a comfortable but lovely Victorian manner with a beautiful side garden, which can be used for receptions and meetings and also contains a Civil War display honoring both Confederate and Union soldiers; the Carteret County Jail (c. 1829), architecturally perfect, containing two cells and jailkeeper's quarters and used as the county jail until 1854; Apothecary's Shop and Doctor's Office (c. 1859), which displays appropriate furnishings and many original articles and examples for instruments, bottles, and prescriptions used in early county medicine.

Ocracoke Island

Number of miles:	27.4 (30.4 with optional trip to light-house)
Approximate pedaling time:	2½ hours
Terrain:	Flat
Traffic:	Heavy right after ferries land and during peak summer months
Things to see:	Village of Ocracoke, Ocracoke Lighthouse, Cape Hatteras National Seashore, natural sights
Food:	Lots of options in Ocracoke Village, vending machines at ferry terminals

This rustic island village charms visitors with its narrow, curving, sandy streets reminiscent of old-world Europe. Known primarily as a center for fishing and bird hunting, Ocracoke more recently has begun to attract tourists, thanks to a large new hotel. Fortunately it still retains its rustic charm, and you'll enjoy cycling through the village, built around Silver Lake, if you choose to visit the Ocracoke Lighthouse, called in one guide "a photographer's dream." This lighthouse is the oldest still in service in North Carolina. The infamous pirate Blackbeard (Edward Teach) met his death in Silver Lake Harbor in 1718.

Ocracoke has always been one of the most isolated island communities because it is accessible only by ferry. Linguists have studied the English spoken by the natives because their isolation helped them retain portions of the Elizabethan accent used by their forebears.

After you leave the village of Ocracoke, you'll enter the Cape Hatteras National Seashore marked by grass marshes, low scrub

trees, and clusters of pines. Just outside of the village, NC–12 sports modest shoulders for cyclists to allow motorists to pass more safely. The beaches on this island are among the least populated and most beautiful of the National Seashore. If you want to swim, be wary of the strong tides and currents characteristic of this seashore. There are no lifeguard stations and very few people to help if you run into trouble.

A must-see is the Ocracoke Pony Park at 7.7 miles. These ponies, which used to roam wild about the island, are direct descendants of the Spanish mustangs that have long inhabited the island. Concern for the safety and well-being of the ponies led the government to create a fenced pasture for them in the park.

Throughout the National Seashore, watch for dwarf, misshapen trees, which the strong, salt-laden winds have pruned into unusual shapes. The violent storms that periodically batter the island continually recreate the shoreline, removing sand from one side and redepositing it elsewhere. Historical maps of the Outer Banks illustrate how new inlets are created and others closed as the result of these storms. Such change makes these barrier islands a dynamic part of our natural world.

A myriad variety of birds and ducks populate the island or use its beaches and marshes for their twice-yearly migrations. Birding is popular here in the fall and spring during migrating seasons and also in the winter. Snow geese, Canada geese, and a variety of ducks are common sights at these times. Besides the plentiful gulls and plovers, it's not uncommon to see white herons and great white egrets in the marsh areas. Sandpipers and rails fascinate with their rapid scurrying on the sand and quick beaks for elusive sea creatures that have washed ashore. There's always plenty to see and learn on the coast. And, if you're lucky, you might see a family of dolphins playing and splashing just beyond the breakers.

Lighthouse Option
OCRACOKE VILLAGE DETAIL

Ferry office

★ **START**
public parking

12

Silver Lake Rd.

To Island Tour

Ocracoke
Lighthouse

Point Rd.

Creek Rd.
1327

12

NORTH

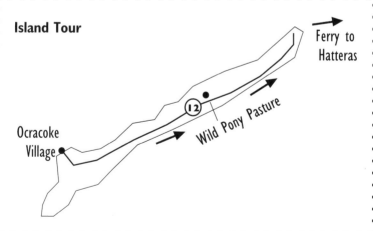

Island Tour

Ferry to
Hatteras

12

Wild Pony Pasture

Ocracoke
Village

DIREC-TIONS at a glance

0.0 From edge of Ocracoke Village Visitor's Parking Lot (just to left as you exit ferry), turn left on the main street.

0.4 Turn left onto NC–12.

7.7 Turn left into Ocracoke Pony Park. Upon exiting turn left onto NC–12.

13.8 Arrive at ferry terminus for Hatteras ferry (*see* Ride 39, "To the Lighthouse"). Turn around and retrace route along NC–12.

27.2 Bear right on main street in Ocracoke Village toward ferry terminal.

27.4 Return to parking lot.

Optional Side Trip to Ocracoke Lighthouse

0.8 Turn right off NC–12 onto Silver Lake Road.

1.2 Turn left onto Creek Road (SR 1327).

1.4 Turn right onto Point Road.

1.5 Arrive at lighthouse. Turn around and retrace route back to NC–12.

2.2 Bear left onto NC–12 to return to starting point or turn right onto NC–12 to resume main ride at 13.8 miles.

Getting There

To get to Ocracoke, you must take either Cedar Island or Swan Quarter ferry from the mainland, the ride on each of which lasts more than two hours. The cost is $2.00 for a bicycle and rider; $10.00 for a passenger vehicle up to 20 feet in length. Reservations are a must during peak summer months. From the north you can take free ferry from Hatteras Island, accessible by car via NC–12 from Nags Head and Manteo. Parking lot where ride starts is adjacent to ferry terminal in Ocracoke village.

To the Lighthouse:
Hatteras Island

Distance:	25.4 miles
Approximate pedaling time:	2½ hours
Terrain:	Flat, but windy
Things to see:	Cape Hatteras National Seashore, Cape Hatteras Lighthouse, Atlantic Ocean, wide variety of shorebirds
Food:	Small stores and restaurants in Frisco and Buxton

Hatteras Island is one of the longest of North Carolina's barrier islands known as the Outer Banks. Thanks to its designation as part of the Cape Hatteras National Seashore, most of the island retains the appearance it must have had when British immigrants first settled here more than three hundred years ago.

The natural sights are the biggest attraction for tourists. As you pedal along the relatively smooth asphalt of NC–12, you'll find mile upon mile of sandy beaches, unmarred by billboards, high-rise hotels, and thousands of sun worshippers. Instead, there's the constant sound of the wind and the ocean, broken by the cries of gulls and swoosh of wings as herons and egrets take flight. It's not unusual to see bottlenose dolphins playing in the water near the shore. Because these lands are public property, visitors have free access to the beach, but it's best to use the marked trails in order to preserve the fragile vegetation that is critical to preventing erosion.

Because most of the island is natural—that is, "undeveloped," it's important to plan ahead regarding water and other supplies. Water and limited refreshments are available at the ferry terminal, but the next supplies aren't available until you

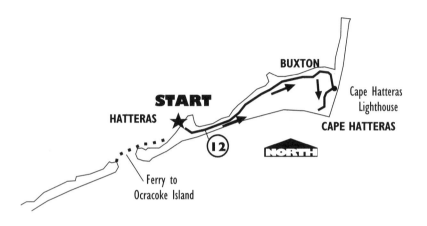

Getting There

Ride starts near southernmost end of Hatteras Island, which can be reached by free ferry from Ocracoke Island or by driving south from Nags Head along NC–12.

DIRECTIONS at a glance

0.0 From parking lot at ferry landing, turn left onto NC–12.

2.7 Enter Cape Hatteras National Seashore.

4.2 Arrive at Regional beach access (rest rooms available).

4.6 Pass Cape Hatteras pier.

8.7 Enter Buxton.

12.0 Turn right into Cape Hatteras Lighthouse National Park.

12.9 Turn left into lighthouse parking lot. Turn around and retrace route.

25.4 Return to ferry landing.

reach Frisco or Buxton. The flat terrain makes cycling look really easy, but strong headwinds are common and can be worse than long hills because there's no letup.

This part of North Carolina has much to recommend it. Historically this stretch of coast has been known as the Graveyard of the Atlantic because the convergence of waters to the south and from the north of the cape make it particularly rough during storms. More than six hundred ships have wrecked here—perhaps because of the shallow shoals or storms and some because of war. During World War II German submarines sank so many Allied tankers and cargo ships here that the waters became known as Torpedo Junction.

The Cape Hatteras Lighthouse, like many others, was vital to warning ships of the dangerous Diamond Shoals just off shore and directing them to land. Built in 1870, it stands 208 feet, the tallest in the United States. Since the 1980s, the light has been the center of a controversy because shifting sands have eroded much of the beach to the east of it. Some preservationists have suggested building a seawall to protect the light while others are trying to raise money to move the lighthouse farther from the ocean. For the moment, sand dumped between the lighthouse and the sea has stabilized it, but visiting hours are restricted because of its precarious situation.

At the lighthouse station are exhibits about the area, including information about the lifesaving endeavors and the large number of ships that have sunk off shore. A park ranger presents talks on different topics during the peak summer tourist season. A self-guiding nature trail begins near the lighthouse and is well marked.

The towns on Hatteras sport gray-shingled houses with broad porches, an architectural style typical for the Outer Banks. Outside the National Seashore seafood restaurants and small grocery stores abound, so indulge yourself either before, during, or after your ride. And enjoy the quiet beauty of the Outer Banks.

Blackbeard's Trace:
Bath

Number of miles:	26.3
Approximate pedaling time:	2½ hours
Terrain:	Flat
Traffic:	Light
Things to see:	Historic town of Bath, Goose Creek State Park, rich farmlands
Food:	Refreshments and restaurants in Bath

The notorious pirate Blackbeard, real name Edward Teach, was attracted to the North Carolina coast, especially around Bath, where he lived for a time, because the numerous inlets and coves offered a myriad of hiding places. Blackbeard aside, this quaint and attractive town, North Carolina's first, offers much for the inquiring visitor. Whether you choose to tour or simply stroll along the streets, you'll be captivated by Bath.

Bath was established in 1705. French Protestants from Virginia came first, followed by English settlers, among whom was John Lawson, surveyor general of the colony and author of the first history of Carolina in 1709. By 1708 Bath was inhabited by about fifty people living in twelve houses and surviving through the trade of tobacco, naval stores, and furs. The first public library in the colony was established here in 1701 with the library sent to St. Thomas Parish, which also established a free school for American Indians and blacks. St. Thomas is the oldest existing church in the state.

The North Carolina General Assembly met in Bath in 1743, 1744, and 1752, and the town was considered for colonial capital. However, when the Beaufort County government moved up

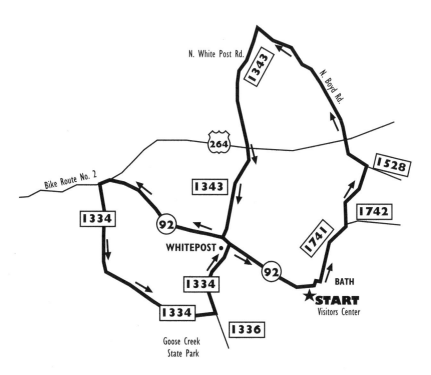

N. White Post Rd.

N. Boyd Rd.

1343

1528

264

Bike Route No. 2

1334

1343

1742

92

1741

WHITEPOST

92

1334

BATH

1334

1334

★START
Visitors Center

1336

Goose Creek
State Park

Getting There

From Washington take U.S. 264 east to
NC–92, which takes you to into Bath.
Visitors Center at Historic Bath State
Historic Site is on south side of NC–92.

DIREC-TIONS at a glance

0.0 From Bath Visitors Center parking lot, turn right onto NC–92
0.1 Turn left onto SR 1741.
1.5 Turn left onto SR 1742.
3.1 Turn left onto North Boyd (SR 1528).
4.0 Cross U.S. 264.
7.6 Turn left onto North White Post Road (SR 1343).
10.6 Cross U.S. 264.
12.9 Turn right onto NC–92.
16.3 Turn left onto U.S. 264.
16.4 Turn left onto SR 1334.
18.9 Arrive Goose Creek State Park.
21.7 Turn left to stay on SR 1334 (SR 1336 goes off to right).
23.8 Turn right onto NC–92.
26.3 Turn right into Bath Visitors Center parking lot.

the Pamlico River to the new town of Washington, Bath lost most of its importance and trade.

Remaining from those early years are some outstanding examples of architecture: St. Thomas Church (1734), the Palmer-Marsh House (1751), and the Van Der Veer House (1790). The Palmer-Marsh House, Bath's oldest residence, was the largest residence in the colonial period and is noted for the windows in its large double chimney. These and other historic sites are open to visitors. During the Civil War Bath was spared from Union occupation so that the town remained intact and ready for more recent restoration efforts. The original town limits are the boundaries of a National Register historic district.

The route from Bath winds through farms and cornfields interspersed with dense forests and small residential communities. Deer frequently graze by the roadside. The flat terrain and smooth road surfaces allow for plenty of looking around. The dark, rich soil in this area bears testament to the inland sea that used to cover this area and left bounteous nutrients for growing a wide variety of crops. A park at Bonner Point on Bath Creek offers picnic tables and a good vantage point of the waterfront.

At 18.9 miles you'll arrive at Goose Creek State Park, which offers rest rooms, swimming, picnic areas, nature study, and camping. The park is situated at the juncture of Goose Creek and the Pamlico River. The route then takes you to the small crossroads of Whitepost and then across the Pamlico River into Bath along NC–92.

Mattamuskeet Meander:
Hyde County

Number of miles:	39.5
Approximate pedaling time:	3 hours
Terrain:	Flat
Traffic:	Light except for U.S. 264, which is major road in area
Things to see:	Lake Mattamuskeet, Lake Mattamuskeet National Wildlife Refuge, Fairfield National Historic District, numerous old homes, sweeping vistas
Food:	Restaurants in Fairfield and Englehard, NCDOT rest area and picnic tables in Englehard

This tour begins on the south side of Lake Mattamuskeet, the largest natural lake in North Carolina, and crosses the lake on NC–94—a North Carolina Scenic Byway, which was built on a causeway bisecting the lake. Wide grassy areas adjacent to the highway attract fishers and boaters to the area but also offer spectacular views. The lake itself is the principal attraction in this area, and its survival to this day is testament to the power of Mother Nature, against whom a great battle was waged in the early 1900s.

At that time Lake Mattamuskeet was purchased, a town called New Holland was established, and canals were built to drain the lake. A pumping station, the world's largest at the time, fueled the drainage. The rich soil at the lake bed could then be farmed. Eventually, however, nature held sway and the lake once again filled with water. In 1934 the lake and surrounding banks became the Lake Mattamuskeet National Wildlife

Refuge. As you enter the refuge proper, at about 2.6 miles, you'll shortly see the entrance to the lodge on your right. The lodge is the former pumping station and has exhibits about the history of the area.

During fall and spring thousands of migratory birds seek haven here: tundra swans, Canada geese, snow geese, and fifteen kinds of ducks. Other birds common to the area include the bald eagle, osprey, great blue heron, common egret, glossy ibis, pileated woodpecker, prothonotary warbler, and indigo bunting. A quiet approach by bike might also allow you to see white-tailed deer, which are plentiful, river otters, muskrats, and perhaps a black bear. It's best to hang food in containers from tree branches away from your person and bike if you're having a picnic.

In the water's shallower edges, you'll see graceful cypress trees with their "knees" sometimes visible just at the surface. Be prepared to wave to locals you pass on these back roads because they'll frequently throw up a hand in greeting as they pass, whether you're on a bike or in a pickup.

Just north of where you turn right on SR 1311 is the town of Fairfield, which has an interesting historic district, if you're inclined to extend your travels a bit. Continuing on your circumnavigation of the lake will take you past several individual historic properties. For example, the George Israel Watson House is located on SR 1116. Several other historic houses line U.S. 264 along the southeastern shore of the lake. Signs near the road give the home's name and its constriction date.

The very flat terrain provides an unusual perspective on wide expanses of corn and other crops, emphasizing the scattered population and the importance of agriculture in this area.

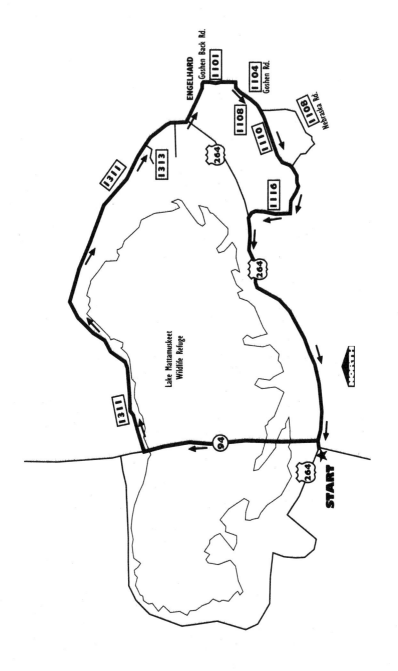

DIREC-TIONS
at a glance

0.0 From Mattamuskeet School parking lot, turn right onto U.S. 264.

0.4 Turn left onto NC–94 and continue across lake.

2.6 Entrance to Wildlife Refuge.

6.6 Turn right onto SR 1311.

20.4 Turn left onto U.S. 264.

21.9 Turn right onto Goshen Back Road (SR 1101).

22.9 Turn left onto Goshen Road (SR 1104).

24.7 Turn left onto SR 1108.

25.1 Turn right onto SR 1110.

29.0 Turn right onto SR 1116.

30.5 Turn left onto U.S. 264.

39.5 Turn left into school parking lot.

Getting There

From Washington, N.C., take U.S. 264 East to Lake Mattamuskeet in eastern North Carolina and park in lot for Mattamuskeet School on south side of U.S. 264 near intersection with SR 1131 and about 0.4 mile west of intersection with NC–94.

Acknowledgments

Many other people helped behind the scenes with suggestions, contributions, encouragement, and support as I worked intensely for six months to meet the publication deadline. Thanks first of all to my family and to Bruce for their unfailing encouragement and support and to my twenty-year-old daughter, Elizabeth, who kept reminding me that she was impressed with this project.

Thanks next to Mary Meletiou of the Office of Bicycle and Pedestrian Transportation in the North Carolina Department of Transportation (NCDOT) for recommending me to the publisher, advising me on routes, and supplying a ton of useful information, not to mention her words of encouragement. She also made available route maps for the following areas, which her office had produced: Swansboro, Transylvania County, Raleigh, High Point, Moore County, Richmond County, and the Lincoln County portion of the North Carolina Bike Route System.

Thanks also to Cynthia Ferguson, Susan Moran, and the staff at the North Carolina Division of Travel and Tourism for making arrangements for accommodations in many of the areas I toured, even when I had to change my travel schedule.

Other thanks to these people and organizations for their help:
- Kathy and David Pounds and Chuck Sams for assisting with photographs.
- Walter Hoover and Diane and Herbert McGuire for their hospitality at the Ivy Terrace Bed and Breakfast Inn in Saluda, a truly outstanding place to stay.
- Clyde and Linda Brooks at the Carolina Maple Getaway in Brevard for their hospitality and for Clyde's route recommendations. I really appreciated their afternoon tea service.
- Carol Lohr from Carteret County for her assistance with accommodations.
- Merrill Stebbins from Transylvania County for arranging accommodations at the Carolina Maple Getaway in Brevard.
- Marla Tambellini from Asheville for reserving hotel accommodations.

- Shannon from Yancey County for making arrangements with the NuWray Inn in Burnsville.
- The Cashiers Area Chamber of Commerce for route maps and recommendations.
- Ellen Sims of Rainbow Cycles in Southern Pines for her recommendations on routes.
- Laurel Stanell of the Moore County Convention and Visitors Bureau for help with reservations and information.
- Bruce Cunningham of Southern Pines for taking time to recommend the tour of Southern Pines and provide historical background, including his special book on the area, and then ride the historical tour route with me.
- Kelley with Bald Head Island Guest Services for her assistance with reservations and information.
- Owen D. Young of the Triad Wheelers Bicycle Club for his recommendations of two routes in Guilford and Rockingham counties.
- Claudia Nix, Barbara Olsen, and the Blue Ridge Bike Club for their suggestions and information for the rides in Asheville and Burnsville.
- Ken Putnam of Ken's Bicycle Shop in Winston-Salem for introducing me to the Fleetwood-to-Todd ride over twenty years ago and then supplying maps and information regarding the Pilot Mountain and Hanging Rock rides. He also kept my bike tuned up for the duration of the tours.
- Mike Boone of Magic Cycles in Boone for recommendations on the route in Valle Crucis.
- Mel Murray for introducing me to the Orton Plantation ride many years ago and then supplying route information for the book.
- Vicki Isley of the Durham Convention and Visitors Bureau for the large packet of information she sent, including information on cycling routes in the area.
- My friend Gene Gillam for accompanying me on the research for the Alamance County ride in the pouring rain and lending me his North Carolina atlas.

- Kenneth J. Tippette of the Down East Cycling Club for his recommendations and accurate, detailed directions for the tours in Bath and around Lake Mattamuskeet.
- Rooney Coffman, my fellow classmate at St. Andrews, for his research and route recommendations for Scotland County.
- Chris Lawrence of Cabella Bicycles in Landrum, South Carolina, for his recommendations for routes in the Polk County area.
- Kimerly Edwards for riding with me on part of the Hunting Country Loop in Polk County, even though my pace was much slower than hers.
- Jacquie Ziller, director of travel and tourism for Polk County, for the maps, information, and reservations at the Ivy Terrace.
- My business partner, Tom Collins, who graciously accepted my early departures on research days and my bleary eyes after nights of working on the text for the book.
- My mother and stepfather, Doris and Harold Lewis, for their lively and informative conversation about the sights along the Hanging Rock and Pilot Mountain rides. Having them along made the research more enjoyable.
- My brother Jim Lawson for gathering maps and information on the Salisbury area for me.
- My special guy, Bruce Heye, who recommended the route in Salisbury. But much more so, he accompanied me on every trip except two, providing sage advice, impeccable sagwagon services, lots of encouragement, wonderful dinner conversation, and just plain fun.

I apologize in advance in case there's anyone I've overlooked. Your efforts, too, were appreciated, even though my feeble brain did not note your contribution.

About the Author

Judi Lawson Wallace bloomed late as a cyclist, getting her own first bicycle at the age of twenty-three, although she had learned to ride as a child. Her cycling career began with using her single-speed bike for transportation in Arizona, Alaska, and North Carolina. She added recreational cycling to her repertoire when she purchased her first ten-speed bike and has toured by bike in Arizona, Florida, Maine, Vermont, New York, South Carolina, Georgia, in the château country of France, and in her native state of North Carolina.

A bicycling activist, she served on the North Carolina Bicycle Committee, advising state government, for seven years, including five as chair of the committee. She received the Sam Thomas Award from the State of North Carolina and the Silver Spoke Award from the North Carolina Bicycle Federation for advocacy of bicycle issues. While a teacher, she developed and taught for four years an award-winning bicycle safety course for fourth and fifth graders at the Summit School in Winston-Salem. She has authored numerous articles on bicycling for popular magazines and professional publications.

The author is a partner in Collins & Wallace, a corporate and marketing communications firm, and also operates her own firm, Wallace Consulting.